# Man Overboard

## INSIDE THE HONEYMOON
## CRUISE MURDER

### JOAN LOWNDS

LYONS PRESS
Guilford, Connecticut
*An imprint of Globe Pequot Press*

To buy books in quantity for corporate use
or incentives, call **(800) 962-0973**
or e-mail **premiums@GlobePequot.com**.

Lyons Press is an imprint of Globe Pequot Press.

Text design: Sheryl Kober
Layout: Justin Marciano
Project editor: Kristen Mellitt

Library of Congress Cataloging-in-Publication Data
Lownds, Joan.
    Man overboard : inside the honeymoon cruise murder / Joan Lownds.
        p. cm.
    ISBN 978-0-7627-7382-4
    1. Missing persons--Turkey. 2. Honeymoons--Turkey. 3. Cold cases (Criminal investigation)--Turkey. 4. Smith, George Allen, 1978- 5. Royal Caribbean Cruise Line. I. Title.
    HV6762.T9L69 2011
    364.152'3092--dc23

                                                                                2011021774

Printed in the United States of America

10 9 8 7 6 5 4 3 2 1

For Kevin

# Contents

*1*  Something Terrible . . . . . . . . . . . . . . . . . 1

*2*  Social Barriers . . . . . . . . . . . . . . . . . . 5

*3*  The Honeymoon Unravels. . . . . . . . . . . . . .13

*4*  Missing . . . . . . . . . . . . . . . . . . . . . .22

*5*  Grim Journey . . . . . . . . . . . . . . . . . . .34

*6*  Fighting Back . . . . . . . . . . . . . . . . . . .37

*7*  Finding a Voice . . . . . . . . . . . . . . . . . .46

*8*  Another Ally. . . . . . . . . . . . . . . . . . . .57

*9*  Scandal Management . . . . . . . . . . . . . . .63

*10*  The Industry. . . . . . . . . . . . . . . . . . . .72

*11*  Strength in Numbers . . . . . . . . . . . . . . .82

*12*  Stormy Waters. . . . . . . . . . . . . . . . . . .97

*13*  In the Vortex. . . . . . . . . . . . . . . . . . . 113

*14*  Out of the Box . . . . . . . . . . . . . . . . . . 123

*15*  Shaken Lives. . . . . . . . . . . . . . . . . . . 142

*16*  Mounting Pressures . . . . . . . . . . . . . . . 158

*17*  Court Drama . . . . . . . . . . . . . . . . . . . 182

*18*  Glimmers of Hope. . . . . . . . . . . . . . . . . 201

# Something Terrible

In the predawn hours of July 5, 2005, the *Brilliance of the Seas* luxury Royal Caribbean cruise ship sailed at nine knots toward Kuşadasi, Turkey. With 2,500 passengers onboard, it cut a wide, glittering swath through the dark waters of the Aegean. The opulent 962-foot, 90,090-ton ship is a floating city, with four-star restaurants, bars, a casino, a health club, and a hair salon. Glass elevators glide up the thirteen decks, an indoor waterfall cascades behind a curved staircase, and sixteen-foot stone elephants flank an Indian-themed solarium with hot tubs and a swimming pool.

That night the clear sky burned with stars that sizzled above the calm sea. Waves lapped against the sides of the boat. In the distance shone the lights of a passing ship. Gradually the darkness thinned to gray as the first fingers of daylight pierced the mist. The ship sailed closer to land, and a pale sliver of beach along Turkey's coast came into view.

Above the pristine sands the faint outlines of olive groves, rocky crags, and pinewoods stirred with birdsong.

One of the first passengers to wake that morning was sixteen-year-old Emilie Rausch from Chicago. She eagerly anticipated the day's excursion—a tour of the ruins of Ephesus, just outside Kuşadasi, one of the best-preserved cities of the ancient world. She had a new digital camera for the trip, which she brought with her when she stepped outside her cabin door to watch the sunrise. As the sea shimmered with the first blush of light, she snapped a few shots. Then she took a walk along the ship, climbing from her deck, 7, to Deck 9. The drone of the engine and the shrieking of black-backed gulls were the only sounds at that early hour. She watched the light turn gold, flickering across the water like rows of votive candles. The Windjammer cafe was preparing breakfast—eggs for the omelet station, bacon, and ham—the aromas wafting on the breeze.

As Emilie took the stairs back down to Deck 7, she noticed something jarring—a blotchy red stain stretching several feet on the wide metal overhang protecting the lifeboats. She looked closer.

It was blood.

Red handprints marked a path over the side of the ship. Her heart pounded, and her idyllic mood that morning turned to terror.

Emilie snapped pictures of the bloody scene then, frightened, ran back to her cabin and showed the gruesome photographs to her mother, Barbara McCulloch. As Barbara scrolled through them, she remembered hearing a woman's scream coming from the direction of the Smith cabin the previous night. She called ship security.

Meanwhile, Walter Zalisko, from Jersey City, New Jersey, was awakened at 6:30 a.m. by his cousin, who noticed the long, bloody stain on her way to breakfast. Viewing the horrific scene, the thirty-two-year police veteran immediately recognized it as something he had seen too many times back home.

"This is not an accident," Zalisko told his cousin. The size and placement of the railings made it impossible to fall overboard by chance. The deep red of the stain was consistent with blood from a violent head injury, and he estimated that it consisted of about two pints, dripping down the overhang.

Ship officials began a frantic search of the cabins in the area near the bloodstain. The Smith cabin was vacant, with reports of blood inside, starting on the rug.

Jennifer and George Smith, a couple on their honeymoon from Connecticut, were paged over the public address system. News of George's disappearance sent shockwaves across the ship. "The rumor mill started flying," recalled passenger Linda Bruck. By the time the ship reached its final destination in Naples, Italy, four days later it had become known as the "ship of terror."

Ship officials found Jennifer receiving a massage in the Ship Shape Center. The massage had been scheduled as a couples massage for her and George, but she was alone. She reportedly had arrived an hour and a half early, without her husband and, despite a penchant for dressing meticulously, wearing the same dress she had worn the night before.

"Your husband has gone missing," a ship official told her. She immediately called her parents back home in Connecticut. She asked to call the Smith family, too, but she claims she was not allowed to do so by ship officials.

Crewmembers escorted her to the ship's main lobby for questioning. Surrounded by glass walls that afforded shimmering views of the sea, Jennifer was questioned about the disappearance of her husband by Turkish police. She was soon joined by the four men last seen with George—three Russian Americans living in New York and a man from California.

While the interrogation took place, John Hagel, Jennifer's father, called the Smith family in Greenwich, Connecticut. George's mother, Maureen Smith, was making coffee and looking forward to spending the summer day with relatives still in town from the wedding festivities. Perhaps they'd visit one of the Greenwich beaches.

At 6:30 a.m. John Hagel's words shattered her world: "Maureen, something terrible has happened to George," he said, choking out the words between sobs.

Her pulse raced with rising panic. Maureen set the phone down carefully and started to pray. *Please God, let my son live. Let him live.* Then her doorbell rang, and reporters started to gather on her lawn.

The media circus had begun.

## 2

# SOCIAL BARRIERS

Greenwich, Connecticut, a privileged enclave on Fairfield County's gold coast, spans miles of shoreline along Long Island Sound. The Manhattan skyline is visible from Greenwich Point, one of the town's magnificent beaches. In the center of town, Greenwich Avenue gleams with tony stores such as Saks Fifth Avenue, Tiffany's, Best and Co., J. Crew, and Brooks Brothers. During winter, women shop here dressed in fur coats. Greenwich police officers are stationed at the intersections as a courtesy to help pedestrians navigate across the street.

When George Smith IV met Jennifer Hagel, he tried to bridge the gap between his wealthy, sheltered Greenwich world and blue-collar Cromwell, Connecticut, where she grew up as a cop's daughter in a house not far from the neon bleed of eateries and no-tell motels on the Berlin Turnpike. He also tried to cross a wider, perhaps unbridgeable, divide between the differences in their personalities. But the "good boy" from Greenwich fell suddenly and profoundly in love with the flirtatious Cromwell girl, who liked the attention of men. She was different from the Greenwich women he usually dated, according to his friends, and there was a powerful attraction between them.

Born on October 3, 1978, George grew up in Glenville, Connecticut, on the outskirts of town, near the border with Rye, New York. He and his older sister, Bree, were raised by their father, George III, and their red-haired mother, Maureen Walsh Smith. Maureen grew up in Hertfordshire, just outside London, raised by Irish-born parents, while the Smith family had lived in Greenwich for generations. George I pitched for the Brooklyn Dodgers during World War I, returning home to teach math at Greenwich High School; George II bred horses and was a dentist, dispensing free dental care to those who couldn't afford it.

George III and Maureen owned Cos Cob Liquors, a popular mom-and-pop liquor store, and the oldest in Greenwich, on the Post Road overlooking Strickland Brook Park. George IV had planned to take over the store after his father retired.

"Everyone has always had nothing but the best regard for the Smith family," said town resident Mickey Sherman, former CBS legal analyst and defense lawyer. "They had the best reputation—nice people, active in the community. No one would have anything negative to say about them."

In the comfortable family home, with its spacious yard, basketball hoop, outdoor grill, and mixed-breed dog, George grew up surrounded by his family's love and suburban peace and order. His parents shuttled him to Cub Scout meetings, football practice, PTA picnics, and church groups, and both parents took active roles in their children's upbringing.

Among the many family photographs in the living room are pictures of George as a sturdy blond toddler, then at his high school graduation. Another shows the family of four a few years before George's wedding, smiling broadly aboard the same *Brilliance of the Seas* that would turn to catastrophe for their son, dressed formally for the ship's elegant restaurant. The last photo shows George as a tall, handsome, dark-haired groom, dancing with his mother at his wedding. The pictures form a perfect, tragic timeline of his life.

At Greenwich High, where his great-grandfather had taught math, the six-foot-four teen was a star linebacker on the football team. After graduating in 1996, he went to Babson College outside Boston, where he studied computer science, pledged Tau Kappa Epsilon, and earned a business degree.

Shawn Keenan, who lived two doors down in the dorm at Babson, lifted weights with George almost every day. "George was one of those guys that in a group situation had a tough exterior, but he definitely liked being around people. When you got him one on one, he definitely would talk more than he would reveal to anyone in a group situation, so we got to talk a lot," Keenan said to Dennis Murphy on *Dateline NBC*'s "Disappearance Before Dawn" in September 2005. "He was just the kind of guy who liked to have a lot of fun, kind of a prankster. Not the class clown or anything, but he definitely liked to have fun with all the guys on the floor."

Under his picture in the Babson yearbook is a quote from an Ella Wheeler Wilcox poem:

> 'Tis the set of the sails and not the gales
> which tell us the way to go.

It proved eerily prophetic.

After graduation, George took a job with a computer company in Stamford, Connecticut, doing research on Internet search engines. He later moved to a similar firm in suburban Boston. George surprised the family in 2003 by quitting his job and coming back to work at the liquor store. "It was the pull of family, absolutely the pull of family," said his boss at the time, Amanda Watlington.

George's outgoing personality wasn't suited to computer work. "At his job he worked at a desk from eight to six every day, and he said he couldn't sit in front of a computer anymore," said his mother.

"He needed more social interaction," added Bree.

George moved into an apartment in Byram, close to Cos Cob, and set to work creating a website for the family store. He lifted weights every day, ran, and rode his bike to work in warm weather along the hilly streets. His athletic looks attracted a following of young women in the store. "I used to go in there just to see him because he was so handsome and just as nice as he was handsome," one woman recalled.

A serial monogamist, he was enjoying a bachelor's life, taking wine study courses and planning tastings, when he met Jennifer Hagel on a summer day in Newport, Rhode Island.

———

Suburban blue-collar Cromwell lies about a ninety-minute drive from Greenwich into the heart of Connecticut, south of Hartford and northeast of New Haven. But the socioeconomic gap between the two towns is much wider. In 2006 the per capita income in Greenwich was $74,346, more than double Cromwell's $32,750.

Cromwell's "miracle mile" offers a sharp contrast to Greenwich Avenue. On the main drag you will find a Dairy Queen Chill and Grill, a Super 8 Motel, a dollar store, a Burger King, a psychic, and a Caribbean tanning salon. Driving on Cromwell streets, instead of Lincoln Navigators with Obama bumper stickers, are Dodge Ram pickup trucks with American flag decals.

The town is best known for the Tournament Players Golf Club at River Highlands, a stop on the PGA Tour, on the outskirts of town. Jennifer grew up in Cromwell with older sister, Jessica, and younger brother, John. Their father, John, served as a police sergeant and became a private contractor after retiring. Their mother, Debbie, stayed at home to raise the children and later started a real estate business.

In the 1997 Cromwell High School yearbook, Jennifer looks like a cheerleader, with a halo of platinum-blond hair and impeccable makeup. More than just a pretty face, she excelled at varsity soccer, basketball, and golf all four years. Although petite and delicate looking, Jennifer was so fiercely competitive that she was known as "the secret weapon on the intramural softball team," recalled teammate Kara Klenk on *Dateline NBC*'s "Disappearance Before Dawn." To her teammate, it came as no surprise that Jennifer married a fellow jock.

A good student, Jennifer attended Trinity College, a small liberal arts college in Hartford, where she prepared to become an elementary school teacher. After graduating, she attended Roger Williams College in Bristol, Rhode Island, and earned a master's degree in education. At the time, her brother John lived in a summer rental downstairs from George, who was taking a summer vacation from working at his parents' liquor store.

On June 8, 2002, John introduced Jennifer to George, and "we fell quickly in love," Jennifer said. The popular young bachelor never strayed after meeting Jennifer, whom he considered his soul mate. His family noticed the transformation. They said that they could tell he was in love and wanted to settle down. He was a very attentive boyfriend and would stop at Whole Foods on his way home from work to buy salmon, Jennifer's favorite, and grill it for her.

She was different from the more conservative Greenwich women George had been dating, observed Drew Lufkin, one of his fraternity brothers. George, who had been content as a bachelor, had suddenly switched course and was making long-term plans soon after meeting her. He had fallen—hard. "Right from the start they were having long-term plans," said Lufkin, "and I think she got George thinking it was time to settle down. When we were just out of college, we were very happy being bachelors."

But ominous signs had surfaced already. Jennifer's jealousy, Lufkin believed, indicated "an element of trust that was missing on her side. George missed my bachelor party in Las Vegas because Jen wouldn't let him go. If we didn't plan his bachelor party in Miami on our own, then she would have tried to stop him from having it."

The new couple soon settled into a garden apartment in Greenwich next door to the house where his father grew up. George continued working at his parents' store, planning to take over the business so that his father could retire. Jennifer was working as a substitute teacher and trying to find a permanent position in a local elementary school. The two former athletes made a striking pair.

On Valentine's Day 2004, after asking John Hagel for his daughter's hand in marriage, George proposed. Jennifer landed a job teaching third grade in nearby Westport soon thereafter. Their futures secure, the couple began to plan their wedding and envisioned starting a family. George shared Jennifer's love of children, and Jennifer recalled their plans "to have at least two. If we had a boy, which we both secretly hoped for, we would name him George V of course."

The couple chose to have their wedding at the Castle Hill Inn in Newport, where they had met, and invited 150 family members and friends. Despite the apparently idyllic circumstances of their new life together, George began experiencing anxiety. He saw Dr. Stephen Cooper, a psychiatrist in Greenwich, who diagnosed him as suffering from mild anxiety with some symptoms of obsessive-compulsive disorder. Dr. Cooper prescribed a low dose of Zoloft and clonazepam and reported positive results, saying that George was responding well, with no side effects. George was "cured," as Jennifer put it, before the couple went on their honeymoon. He never took more than the prescribed amount of medication, but he did mix the pills with alcohol, she later said in testimony.

As their wedding day approached, George planned their honeymoon, taking meticulous care with every detail. He chose a romantic cruise aboard Royal Caribbean's *Brilliance of the Seas*. The ship departed from Barcelona, with glamorous ports of call in the French Riviera, Rome, and the Greek islands. For their twelve-day honeymoon, George booked a $10,000 package in a midship stateroom, portside on Deck 9, Cabin 9062. It led to a balcony where the newlyweds could watch the ocean glide by at night.

## 3

# THE HONEYMOON UNRAVELS

On Saturday, June 25, 2005, George awoke at his family's Newport home, not far from Cliff Walk, filled with seascapes and surrounded by his mother's gardens, where the family had spent so many happy vacations. He donned his gray tuxedo morning coat with a lily of the valley boutonniere, and slid into the black limousine with his family. They drove past the famous seaside mansions—Rosecliff and The Breakers, where the 1974 Robert Redford film *The Great Gatsby* was filmed— and wound along the hairpin turns of Ocean Drive, past sweet-smelling hedges and blue hydrangeas, to a peninsula with a sweeping view of the water.

Castle Hill Inn—a classic New England seaside resort voted one of the "Best in the World" by *Condé Nast Traveler* and visited often by playwright Thornton Wilder—features perennial gardens, walking trails that slope down to Narragansett Bay, and a private beach. On a hilltop beside gardens covered with sea roses and goldenrod, George and Jennifer were married.

She wore a strapless lace wedding gown and carried a bouquet of white roses and lilies. After the ceremony, bagpipes played in honor of the mother of the groom. The bride and groom danced to their song: "Into the Mystic" by Van Morrison. Everyone described the wedding as idyllic. "It was just the perfect day. It was magical. Our parents were just beaming," Jennifer recalled.

"The wedding was gorgeous," Bree said. "It was nicer than you would see in the bridal magazines, the most beautiful couple you can imagine, just everything done to perfection."

"He was just so happy," Maureen remembered wistfully.

On their wedding night, the couple stayed in the Castle Hill Inn wedding suite. They watched beams from the historic lighthouse cut silent arcs through the sky and listened to the chiming of the sea buoys that Wilder so beautifully described in his novel *Theophilus North*.

They had lunch the next day with the Smiths at the family's home in Newport before departing on their honeymoon.

Etched permanently in Maureen's memory is the image of her son waving good-bye, his blue eyes bright with happiness. "He just wanted to get on the plane, just so excited," she recalled. "He couldn't wait to get on that cruise ship. He had planned it night after night."

——

Half the exterior walls on *Brilliance of the Seas* are made of glass, and rising to all nine decks is the futuristic *Spiral Light*, an enormous stainless-steel sculpture. Resembling a white tornado, it casts patterns of swirling, stormy light on a white wall over the Champagne Bar. Though they didn't know it at the time, its ominous shadows perfectly set the stage for George and Jennifer as they boarded the ship in Barcelona on June 29.

The emotional maelstrom that would tear them apart was not yet apparent on the first day of the cruise. In a photo of them standing on the dock in Barcelona, George is wearing a white T-shirt and black shorts, while Jennifer is dressed in a pink-striped shirt and white shorts, leaning into her new husband, who has wrapped his arm securely around her. They are smiling happily, on the cusp of a new life together. Beside them is a promotional poster for *Brilliance of the Seas* with images from its ports of call: the Leaning Tower of Pisa, Greek ruins, an Italian gondola, and an old-fashioned pocket watch, its hands frozen in time.

The luxurious ship thrilled the newlyweds, featuring every amenity and luxury imaginable. Nautical blues and greens made up the decor, and the carpets were stitched with sailing masts and ropes. Gleaming, handcrafted balustrades and wood paneling lined every deck, which teemed with murals, mosaics, statues, and sculptures.

The Smiths' cabin featured a king-size bed and a large marble bath. The furnishings were done in maple wood trimmed with mahogany, and the color scheme, like the rest of the ship, was lush nautical blues, greens, and coppers. The far wall, made of glass, led to a furnished balcony overlooking the ocean.

George and Jennifer settled into a pleasurable routine. George, ever the fitness junkie, worked out every day in the Ship Shape Fitness Center, an ocean-view gym that featured a 200-foot climbing wall, miniature golf course, and jogging track where he ran his daily laps. Afterward he joined Jennifer at one of the ship's pools on Deck 11—the open-air pool, where a live three-piece band often played, or the solarium pool with its enormous plaster elephants, where bird and animal sounds echoed through towering tropical plants. Poolside, Jennifer wore a revealing black bikini, and George displayed his toned, athletic physique.

"At the pool, Jennifer stood out because she was a very beautiful young woman," Walter Zalisko said to the *Greenwich Citizen*. Also memorable to Zalisko were rumors among passengers that George had claimed to have $50,000 of wedding money onboard.

When the ship docked at ports of call, such as Nice, Monaco, Florence, and Rome, Jennifer and George went touring or browsed the stylish European boutiques, indulging their mutual love of shopping. At night the young couple dressed formally to dine in the ship's Minstrel Dining Room or Chops Grille steakhouse. Then they headed to the ship's casino to play blackjack and stopped for a nightcap at the Starquest Disco.

For the first few days, the trip lived up to George's expectations. He sent an e-mail to his family back home in Greenwich. "I'm having such a good time," it read, "please don't contact me until the end of the world, or someone dies."

George and Jennifer befriended a group of young men on the cruise, all in their early twenties. Two brothers, Russian-born Gregory and Zachary Rozenberg, were naturalized American citizens living in Brooklyn with their cousin Rostislav "Rusty" Kofman. Josh Askin, from Paramount, California, south of Los Angeles, was onboard with his family, celebrating his parents' twenty-fifth wedding anniversary.

Royal Caribbean reportedly had warned some of these men about their "inappropriate conduct," such as using profanity and trying to sneak their own alcohol into the disco. A young woman interviewed for *Dateline NBC*'s "Disappearance Before Dawn" remembered them attempting to "pick fights and stealing liquor from the ship's bar."

The two health-conscious former athletes were not heavy drinkers back home. But, as is typical on cruise ships, the alcohol was flowing freely. George and Jennifer joined the hard partying with the four young men, and it soon became volatile.

Less than a week after George's upbeat e-mail to his family, the newlyweds' photographed smiles had faded noticeably. From the photos, it is easy to imagine that conflict marred their last outing together. On Mykonos in Greece on July 4, the last day of his life, George stands before whitewashed cliff houses overlooking the Aegean. A faint, perfunctory smile has replaced his wide grin, and his eyebrows are lifted quizzically. Jennifer is no longer leaning into him; there is a physical gap between them, a void. It is one of the last photographs taken of George, shortly before the couple toured the legendary party island, where in Greek mythology Zeus slew the Titans, the large rocks scattered about the island said to be their petrified corpses.

As they wound through narrow lanes and toured the bucolic scenery, tensions bristled between them. The conversation had dried up, and perhaps doubts were germinating in George's mind. On Kastro hill lies a complex of churches known collectively as Our Lady of Paraportiani. One whitewashed chapel is dedicated to the safety of those who travel at sea. George knelt in a pew and said a prayer for his family.

While drinking beer and eating pita at an outdoor cafe, the couple spotted celebrity Tara Reid filming a segment for her television show, *Wild on Mykonos*. George asked the blond star if he could have his picture taken with her. We can only imagine how Jennifer might have responded, given her possessiveness of George, as reported by George's friend, Lufkin.

The couple then rented mopeds and rode, without helmets, through the winding green hills. As they rounded a bend, a rickety tour bus came barreling toward them; to avoid a collision, they had to jump off the mopeds. "We had to leave the mopeds or we were going to die," Jennifer said. "We were shaken up."

---

After returning to the ship that night, the couple partied harder than ever. They had dinner in the formal Chops Grille dining room. George wore a pink silk tie that matched the pink shirt under his gray jacket, stylish but conservative. Jennifer wore a low-cut black dress with pearls. As they ate, they listened to the tumble and splash of a waterfall behind the staircase. Despite the luxurious setting, uneasiness hung in the air.

After dinner, they headed to the casino for some low-stakes gambling. A gold, life-size statue of the Roman goddess Fortuna Bona stood in the center of the room among all the lights, bells, and whistles inviting passengers to spend their money.

Here George and Jennifer met up with the four young men they had befriended. The liquor was flowing as the group played craps and blackjack in the casino, awash in the plinking, bonging, and bleeping of the swindle machines. They also began drinking shots of absinthe, a strong herbal liqueur not allowed on cruise ships, which one of the group members reportedly had brought onboard after the ship docked in Florence. Reputedly though not actually hallucinogenic, many variations of absinthe do contain 90 percent alcohol, which makes for a fast journey to intoxication.

Witnesses say crewmembers gave George and his companions shot glasses for the absinthe, breaking ship's rules. As the evening wore on, George reportedly became visibly inebriated, but no crewmember contacted a bridge officer, also a violation of Royal Caribbean company policy.

While George was doing shots and his night began to blur, Lloyd Botha, the assistant casino manager, arrived on the scene.

Several passengers said he flirted with Jennifer, and she sat close beside him on a couch, according to Keith Greer, lawyer for Josh Askin, on *Dateline NBC*'s "Disappearance Before Dawn." The group remained in the casino until it closed at 2:00 a.m. and then decided to go to the ship's Starquest Disco.

The five men found seats at a table, where they continued drinking. Passengers said they saw Jennifer again join Botha on a couch. George stood up and approached her. "You hussy," he reportedly said, using a surprisingly old-fashioned term.

Jennifer's reaction was anything but old fashioned. The former varsity soccer player shoved her husband, straightened, and then drop-kicked him in the groin, according to an AP report in January 2006. George bent over in severe pain, according to two eye witnesses. Dominick Mazza said Jennifer "kicked him in the privates and stumbled out of the bar." Another witness, Margarita Chaves, added, "I was very surprised by their behavior, that a honeymoon couple would act that way. His pupils were dilated. I'll never forget the look in his eyes."

Chaves said that Jennifer was "flirting" with a male passenger and that she had been afraid "a fight would start," according to the AP. However, Mazza said that he didn't think Jennifer was flirting, only leaning on the man because she was "drunk."

The kick left George doubled over in pain, Mazza told the AP. "He bent over for a quite a while. You could tell the kick was hard. That was not fooling around."

Jennifer described these reports as "outlandish" and "ridiculous." She told the AP, "That's the epitome of what I've had to deal with. That's not something I would do to my husband."

Reeling, George watched helplessly as Jennifer stormed out of the casino with Botha close on her heels, according to Askin's lawyer, Keith Greer, on the CBS show, *48 Hours Mystery's* "Love Lost," which aired in April 2006. "Josh recalls that they left the disco together," Greer said.

Botha's lawyer, Andrew Rier, denied that his client left with Jennifer, as did Royal Caribbean, through spokesman Greg McCrary.

George stayed in the casino, finishing another shot, perhaps trying to blot out the ugly scene. Then he made his way back to his cabin, accompanied by the Rozenbergs, Kofman, and Askin.

At 3:30 a.m. the group found the Smith cabin dark and empty, surreal after all those months of careful saving and planning. Dejected, George asked his companions to help him find Jennifer, and they set off on a futile search in the hollow, early morning. After half an hour, they gave up, and, according to Greer, all five men returned to George's cabin.

# 4

# MISSING

The disturbance woke passengers in the adjoining cabins. Clete Hyman, a deputy police chief, said he heard what sounded like a college drinking game progress into an argument, raucous noise coming from both the cabin and balcony. It sounded to him as though furniture was being moved, according to *Dateline NBC*'s "Disappearance Before Dawn."

At 4:05 a.m. Hyman banged on the cabin door and called security, which reportedly did not arrive until nearly a half hour later. Meanwhile the noise escalated, now sounding like "furniture being thrown against the walls," according to Greg and Pat Lawyer, passengers on the other side of the Smith cabin.

Then came the sound of an unforgettable, horrific thud. "It was so loud, it reverberated throughout our cabin, and it sounded like someone fell out on the balcony," Pat Lawyer recalled.

At approximately 4:30 a.m., ship security arrived and saw what they described as "teens just leaving the vicinity," which they documented in the ship's logs. Greg Lawyer rushed out into the hallway and told them, "Hey, you guys better get in there because that room is trashed." The security officers left without investigating.

The Rozenbergs and Kofman claim they were back in their cabin at 4:30 a.m. They ordered a huge meal from room service, which arrived around 4:45 a.m. They took pictures of the food with a digital camera, which set a date and time stamp on it. They later said this showed they were in their room at that time, according to Albert Dayan, lawyer for Rusty Kofman, on ABC News Primetime, "Honeymoon from Hell: Husband Vanishes at Sea."

Meanwhile, also around 4:30 a.m., crewmembers found Jennifer asleep in a hallway on the other side of the ship, reportedly outside a crew-only room. Gregg McCrary, a Royal Caribbean spokesperson who is also a former FBI profiler overseeing Royal Caribbean's internal investigation, said Jennifer had never returned to the cabin: "Really sort of MIA until she was found at 4:30 that morning." He described her as "inebriated and smelling of alcohol."

Since Jennifer was unable to walk unaided, ship personnel waited with her while two crewmembers went to her cabin in search of George. They couldn't find him. Despite the mounting evidence of foul play and ship policy, which requires that an unconscious passenger be taken to the ship's infirmary for medical evaluation, crewmembers sat her in a wheelchair and brought her back to her empty cabin. When they asked Jennifer where George was, she replied that he sometimes slept in the cabin of other friends, according to Capt. Bill Wright, senior vice president of Fleet Operations for Royal Caribbean, in an interview with the *Greenwich Citizen* in January 2006: "Jennifer said that he might be spending the night in another cabin, as he had done previously." Jennifer denied that she ever made this statement.

In spite of George being missing and reports of blood in the room, the crewmembers dropped Jennifer off in the cabin and left. She fell asleep.

———

Dawn broke. Emilie Rausch discovered the bloodstain and snapped the famous pictures, soon to become critical evidence. Other passengers began to gather beneath the blood-soaked canopy including Zalisko, the vacationing police veteran. After studying the stain and concluding it was most likely evidence of a homicide, Zalisko headed to the ship captain's office. He offered his expertise to assist them. To his astonishment, they declined his help, he said in an interview with the *Greenwich Citizen*.

Soon after, Jennifer woke alone in the cabin. In the wrongful death suit she later brought against Royal Caribbean, she described blood in the room. But that morning she said she didn't notice anything amiss and therefore didn't alert authorities. In later court testimony she claimed that she blacked out the night before and had no memory of events after a certain point in the casino, when the night turned into a blur of "high tables or standing up . . . And I remember just—either getting to a point where I couldn't—I just remember being just tired, or I have to go home, or I'm standing up, but I'm—and then that's it. I literally don't remember."

But Jennifer was alert enough to arrive reportedly an hour and a half early for her couples massage appointment at the ship's spa. She was wearing the dress she had on the night before and flip-flops. "They have me arriving at like 8:30 for a 10:00 massage or something," Jennifer would later say, in her Probate testimony. "So they have me arriving early for my massage. I could guess that—I shouldn't guess—but I could guess that there is a number of reasons I arrived early. Either I'm dumb and just came early, or there's a time change of an hour difference when you go into the next one. George, if there's one thing about him, he was diligent about knowing about time changes. For example, I'm the kind of person that would keep my clocks [turned back] in the fall . . . I'm always late, so I like to keep them like that so I can be on time. Whereas, George, if there's a time change, would change [the clock]. That could be reason. I have no idea why."

Jennifer relaxed and received her massage in the Ship Shape Center, where she was unable to hear her name paged over the ship's loudspeaker. Ship officials came looking for her. "Three Royal Caribbean Cruise line men told me that my husband had gone missing," she recalled in congressional testimony. "When I heard these cruel words, I literally felt my world spinning out of control."

Jennifer claimed she asked if she could call "George's parents immediately. The cruise line told me not to call anybody. However, I couldn't bear the weight of this nightmare alone. Finally the cruise line permitted me to call my family. My mother answered the phone and heard me crying and handed the telephone to my father. He began to wail when he heard George was gone. We did not know what to do or where to turn."

The crew took Jennifer to the crowded main lobby, where Askin, Kofman, and the Rozenbergs soon joined her. "Other passengers were laughing and smiling and milling around," she said.

Josh Askin's father, Jerry, said that when they heard a page for the Smiths around 8:00 a.m., Josh told the room steward, "You should call them and tell them to stop paging George because he really had a lot to drink last night and he's probably sleeping." Jerry Askin said later, on *48 Hours Mystery*'s "Love Lost," that it never occurred to his son that anything was wrong.

They soon learned about the blood on the canopy and that George was missing. "I was absolutely shocked," Jerry Askin said, "because here was somebody who was alive on a honeymoon and then—oh my God—he may be gone."

He also said that Jennifer appeared deeply agitated. "Apparently the staff captain came in and told them that her husband was missing and presumed overboard. My son was sitting right next to her, and she was shaking, and she was crying, and she was absolutely hysterical. . . . And she just said, 'This is like a bad dream.'"

She said she couldn't remember the events of the previous night. Another crewmember took her to an empty cabin, she said in congressional testimony. "I was told to take a shower. I received a tank top, T-shirt, and gym shorts, all with the Royal Caribbean logo splashed across them. Having to wear the cruise line logo humiliated me."

By then the ship had docked in Kuşadasi, and most of the ship's passengers departed for a tour of Ephesus. Turkish authorities boarded *Brilliance of the Seas* and examined the honeymooners' cabin, questioning Jennifer and the four men. Jerry Askin brought his video camera to record the questioning.

The young men said that they walked an intoxicated George back to his room, but they knew nothing of his disappearance. They claimed they were drinking in the ship's bar with George and Jennifer, that she left, and that they helped George to his cabin.

After questioning, police escorted the group to the Turkish police station. Jerry Askin again taped the interrogation and later released portions of the recording to *48 Hours Mystery's* "Love Lost."

The scene shows Josh sitting nervously in a main lobby with the three Russian-American men while the voices of the police, speaking in Turkish, reverberate around him. A translator holds a crying baby on her lap, making her heavily accented English even more difficult to understand. The four young men insisted they had no involvement in George's disappearance, and the interrogation ended.

"What will happen next?" Jerry Askin asked the translator.

"Jennifer Hagel Smith is going to be arrested for murder," the translator said. "There was blood in the cabin."

Jerry Askin's camera captured his son's emotional reaction. "She has no idea what happened! She was with another man, the casino manager, Lloyd. You need to get him in here. I'm not letting her go to jail. I'm not letting her go to jail!"

Jerry Askin led his son away and tried to calm him.

Despite the evidence of these recordings, Royal Caribbean denied that questioning by Turkish authorities ever took place onboard the ship. On *48 Hours Mystery*'s "Love Lost" reporter Hannah Storm said, "According to Royal Caribbean's official statement, Turkish authorities refused the ship's explicit request that the interviews take place on the ship."

To this, Dr. Askin replied, "Who you gonna believe?"

---

Turkish police didn't charge Jennifer with murder, but she described a harrowing ordeal at the hands of Turkish authorities. She claimed in congressional testimony that she was "mocked and taunted" by the police, who also "looked up my shirt and down my pants without taking me to a private examining room." Eventually she was cleared to leave.

When she returned to the ship, she found all her belongings, along with George's, set in a haphazard pile on the dock. Clothes and personal items that couldn't be crammed in suitcases were stuffed into ten souvenir bags, all emblazoned with the Royal Caribbean logo. Her eyes fell on a pair of George's running shoes sticking out of one plastic bag. She realized at that moment that he "would never wear those sneakers again."

Jennifer said she found herself in Turkey with "no money, no plane ticket, no food, nothing. . . . The cruise line did not offer me help with a flight, hotel arrangements, or anything. I could not speak the native language, and I felt abandoned." She described Royal Caribbean's treatment of her as "malicious." Royal Caribbean vehemently denied her account of the events.

Jennifer's father used his credit card to pay for her flight home, she said. "After two long flights, I arrived at JFK and literally collapsed in the arms of my parents."

Later that day, an anxious Josh Askin headed to the pool, presumably to relax in the sun and nurse his hangover. He sat near Margarita Chaves, who had witnessed Jennifer dropkick George in the casino. "It was the room service that saved us," he reportedly said to the startled young school teacher, referring to the digital photos of the hamburgers they had ordered.

News of George's disappearance spread quickly throughout the ship. "I was worried, definitely, that there was some kind of serious foul play," said Karen Drake, a passenger in a cabin across from the Smiths', in an interview with the *Greenwich Citizen*. "Unless you were playing 'King of the World,' you know, it's just not possible to fall over. And there was so much blood. And the distance from his balcony to that deck was not that great, you know, to generate that kind of injury."

The honeymoon cabin, now a possible crime scene, became a source of passenger speculation. That night, Bree said, "The blood on the overhang had been painted over under the supervision of the ship's captain. They claim they washed it away at six at night because people were looking at it. Well, that is a very poor excuse for why they didn't preserve a crime scene."

Zalisko confirmed that the cabin was never sealed off and contained. "The door to the Smith cabin was left wide open, and people were going in and out, cleaning and vacuuming it. They prohibited a complete investigation."

Another passenger, Sheldon Sandler, whose cabin was a few doors down, remembered seeing "someone with a canister, a vacuum cleaner. The door was open, and he was in there with the vacuum cleaner, cleaning. He was sweeping the floor and everything like that." Sandler added: "It was never sealed off. It never had yellow tape on it. It never had Do Not Enter signs on it."

Adding to the confusion was the way Royal Caribbean had launched into full "risk management mode," a common cruise ship protocol designed to protect their public image, according to Brett Rivkind, the Smiths' maritime lawyer. A team of risk management lawyers was flown in from Miami to Turkey, and they reported to the FBI that there was simply "the possibility of a missing guest," despite reports of commotion in the Smith cabin and blood, Rivkind said. Rivkind also said the lawyers interviewed passengers, trying to twist and slant their statements to support the accident or suicide theory they were now trying to float in the press, despite evidence.

According to Rivkind, this was the beginning of "a full-scale public relations campaign to portray George's disappearance as an accident or suicide. Within days, Michael Crye, head of the International Council of Cruise Lines (ICCL), hinted that George's death may have been self-inflicted. "What can the cruise line industry do if a passenger chooses to harm himself?" Crye asked.

Why did Royal Caribbean turn over the investigation of the potential murder of an American citizen to Turkish authorities in the first place? The authorities clearly didn't have an interest in the crime, since it didn't affect "the peace and dignity of the country," as defined by maritime law. Turkish police went to the trouble of going to a Turkish court to receive the authority to conduct the investigation, Rivkind stated, but they "most likely did not have the technological sophistication American authorities possess."

Other vested interests may have been at stake, according to Rivkind. Kuşadasi is the main Aegean port for the cruise industry, where three hundred thousand cruise ship passengers disembark annually. The lucrative cruise market, a boon for the Turkish economy, generated $9.7 billion in revenues in 2006 alone.

While the ship was docked in Kuşadasi, Turkish police conducted a brief inspection of the Smith cabin and canopy and interviewed a few passengers and crewmembers, an investigation that took approximately two hours, Rivkind said. By contrast, an after-the-fact investigation done by famed forensic scientist Dr. Henry Lee in Miami lasted six hours. Turkish police failed to interview key ear witnesses in adjacent cabins, including the Lawyers and the Hymans, Rivkind said. He attributed this haste to the fact that Royal Caribbean did not wish to interrupt its sailing schedule.

During their investigation on the ship, the Turkish police also reportedly did not lock it down, allowing passengers and crew to disembark, perhaps taking critical evidence with them. Later that day, still on schedule, the ship sailed toward Santorini, Greece, the next port of call, with persons of interest still aboard.

As *Brilliance of the Seas* completed its troubled voyage, a young woman on the ship said she had been sexually assaulted by some of the four men last seen with George Smith. Lawyers for the four men claim it was consensual sex, but the FBI reportedly was investigating them for the disappearance of George Smith as well as the alleged assault, according to a *New York Times* article by Alison Leigh Cowan. "The FBI is also looking into a report of the rape of an 18-year-old woman on the ship two days after Mr. Smith disappeared, according to people with knowledge of the investigation," Cowan wrote. "Some of the same passengers who were seen drinking and partying with Mr. Smith and who later helped him back to his room the night he vanished, appear on videotapes of the alleged sexual assault, according to Royal Caribbean, the operator of the cruise."

The day after George Smith's disappearance, as the ship sailed into the twilight, Capt. Michael Lachtaridis made an announcement over the ship's intercom system to reassure the agitated passengers. "The crew and I have been working with local authorities to investigate whether a passenger may have gone overboard last night," he said. "We hope to have the issue resolved shortly. Enjoy the beautiful sunset."

# 5

# Grim Journey

George and Maureen Smith clung to the frail hope that their athletic son, raised on the Connecticut shore, might have swum to safety. Experts told them that sea currents would have pulled him toward the island of Samos. They packed their suitcases, eluded the press camped on their lawn, and boarded a plane for Greece. Bree agreed to handle the media spectacle and continue their search for answers—which was not going well. Neither Jennifer nor her father, John, the former police sergeant, offered to join George and Maureen in their search.

It was high tourist season in Samos, a lush green island of pine forests and olive groves. Through bright, cobblestoned streets blooming with roses, sightseers visited the wine museum, monasteries, and vineyards, snapping pictures of the famous lion in Pythagoras Square. The beaches were crowded, as were the cafes playing Greek music while spiced lamb cooked on spits. Wearing buttons bearing George's picture, now a permanent part of their wardrobe, George and Maureen walked the hills, posting missing person posters.

No one at the island's hospital had seen or heard anything about their son. They headed to the harbor to charter a boat and set out on their grim search. They made a slow path through the pristine waters, navigating between windsurfers and snorkelers.

Once they were past the harbor, the captain gunned the engine, and they roared past channel-marking buoys into the Aegean. The tide was coming in. Black-backed gulls shrieked behind them. They all had loved the sea. It had framed their lives in Greenwich and in Newport. They had salt water in their veins. But now the sea had claimed their son. They hoped against hope to find George somewhere, swimming, floating, relieved as they pulled him onto the boat.

They scanned the water in every direction, straining, squinting into the hot sun. They searched for several hours along the marsh coves and bays, but there was no sign of him. Maureen's heart was sinking. The captain took them to the spot where George probably had vanished, idling the boat in a tiny inlet. He told them they would probably not be able to find his body. "Seventy-five percent of the bodies lost at sea are never recovered," he said, shaking his head sadly. "The sea takes them."

The couple stared into the abyss that had claimed the body of their son and said a silent prayer.

On the way back to the dock, the engine droned, and George and Maureen wept quietly. Their journey had crushed any hopes that their son might still be alive. As they approached the island, the whitewashed bell tower of the monastery of Panagia Spiliani loomed above them. The captain aligned the vessel with the channel markers and cut the engine so that the back fishtailed into the calm of the harbor. In the slower flow, he tossed out the anchor.

When George stepped off the boat, he was so shaken that he couldn't walk. His knees kept collapsing under him. "I had to stand behind him and help push him along," Maureen said. "I had to practically carry him across the street to our hotel."

The loss of his son had brought George III to his knees.

# 6

# FIGHTING BACK

Meanwhile in Greenwich, Bree looked out the front window
at the swarm of television crews and reporters camped on
the lawn. One local reporter had been ringing the doorbell
nonstop. It reverberated through the house.

Relatives were still visiting from England for the wedding.
Bree could hear them sobbing in the den. John Hagel's call
had crashed into their world as well. Even the family dog
sensed a crisis and stayed close to Bree's side.

The advancing media had trampled her mother's carefully
tended garden, and the lives of her conservative family had
become tabloid fodder. The unwanted attention mortified her.
No one in the family had ever been in the news before. They
had lived in the community for generations with an excellent
reputation. Their home, always a sanctuary, was being invaded.

But what Bree felt more than anything was the vivid
absence of her brother, like a hole blasted through the center
of her life. They had been extremely close, and Bree had

been looking forward to her brother's role in the life of her newborn baby.

Bree had a job in Hong Kong as an attorney with an international corporate law firm, but the world of corporate law, with its capital markets, mergers and acquisitions, and intellectual property, was quickly disillusioning her. Her marriage was also rocky. When she came home for George's wedding, she was hoping for support and advice from her family. She never expected that her brother would go missing and that she would have to fend off the press.

She opened the front door and tersely said "No comment" to the television crews and news reporters camped on the lawn. The story, already international in scope, was erupting across the blogosphere, with many speculating about Jennifer's behavior the night George went missing. Television reports repeatedly flashed a video clip of the now-famous honeymooners poolside on *Brilliance of the Seas*, blond Jennifer in a skimpy black bikini, looking up at her handsome, toned husband.

Bree called Royal Caribbean. She spoke to Pamela Powell, supervisor of guest claims, who said that there was no news about George's disappearance and that it was simply an accident. Her tone was matter-of-fact, "business as usual," Bree said. Powell said nothing to Bree about the bloody trail on the overhang and ear-witness accounts of a violent commotion in the cabin.

"My brother is dead and missing, and Royal Caribbean felt that they didn't need to tell us about what happened on that boat," Bree said in an interview with the *Greenwich Citizen.*

Powell told Bree that Royal Caribbean had conducted a search of the ship for George.

"Please, do another," Bree pleaded.

Powell declined because she said a thorough search had already been done.

Bewildered, Bree complained about the lack of information. When Bree hung up the phone, she began to appraise Royal Caribbean's lack of response or support. Why was the cruise line stonewalling them and refusing to provide any information to a grieving family? She had never seen anything like it, and it struck her as callous.

Soon after, her parents returned home, besieged by the media as they struggled up the front steps with their luggage, both devastated by their journey. The family doctor prescribed sedatives, and both of them sat in their chairs for several days, hovering in a twilit world of shock and pain.

Bree, however, refused to let grief hobble her. Seeing her parents in such anguish fueled her determination. She knew she faced a choice. She could stop questioning Royal Caribbean's account, since her brother was missing anyway, or she could try to fight back, to find out why the cruise line was refusing to provide any assistance to her shattered family, compounding the tragedy.

"We are going to fight back," she said. "We are going to find out what is going on and get some answers about what happened to George."

Her declaration roused her father, who suggested they call their congressman, Rep. Christopher Shays, a moderate Republican who once had his headquarters above the Smiths' store.

Bree made the call, and Shays agreed to help. After his office made some inquiries, Dave Parkin, one of Shays's staffers, called back a few hours later. Parkin told Bree about the blood in her brother's room, which stunned her.

"Why didn't Royal Caribbean tell us this?" she asked.

He explained that, from what he had gathered, the cruise line, sailing in the murky waters of international law and under a Bahamian "flag of convenience," had no obligation to release the information. They didn't even have to tell the Smiths that a police investigation had taken place in Turkey.

Bree was astonished. "This was the beginning of a comprehensive cover-up," she claimed. "We were shocked by the fact that Royal Caribbean could get away with telling us so little, not even that a police investigation had occurred."

After further research by Parkin, they discovered that "not only do Royal Caribbean and the other cruise lines not have to tell the families anything, they don't even have to tell the U.S. authorities anything," Bree asserted. "Unbelievable."

The discovery stunned Shays as well. "I was very unhappy and concerned with how the Smith family was treated," he said. "It made my staff and me all the more determined to see justice done."

"I contacted the FBI," Bree said. "If we had not known this information"—the report of the blood in the room—"our approach would likely have been very different. We might even have believed Royal Caribbean's bogus line that George's death was an accident."

That night, Greenwich's local news station, Channel 12, carried the story of George's disappearance, giving Royal Caribbean's version of events. The newscaster described a drunken honeymooner falling overboard accidentally and said the captain had rejected foul play as a cause in the disappearance.

Disgusted at this misinformation, Bree swung into action again, calling the American embassy in Ankara, the Turkish capital. The press office there agreed to "inform the media that foul play had not been overruled by the investigating authorities," Bree recalled.

Royal Caribbean continued to play the accident card to the press. Lynn Martenstein, vice president of communications, repeatedly told the press that George might have "fallen off."

But Royal Caribbean failed to realize the extent of the attention the story would attract. Investigative reporters uncovered accounts of the blood on the overhang, the failure of ship security to enter the cabin after reports of the loud commotion, the cursory investigation by Turkish authorities, and the failure of the ship to be locked down in Kuşadasi.

The Smiths sat in their living room, switching from channel to channel, taking notes. With Royal Caribbean not cooperating, the media was their only source of information. The family was still refusing comment, struggling to comprehend the magnitude of everything that had happened.

But even the *National Enquirer* got in on the act, plastering George IV's picture across its cover.

Jennifer stayed overnight with the Smiths once or twice a week, bringing their son back to life with her presence when she did. But when the Smiths asked Jennifer questions about the night George went missing, she told them the FBI had warned her not to discuss it, a statement that Bree claims was not truthful.

"We found out that they never told her that," Bree said. "I think what was frustrating for my family was that we had been told she had provided a wealth of information to the FBI, and she had not provided a wealth of information to us. And . . . as the parents and sister of the missing and presumably dead passenger, we should know as much as possible."

Jennifer's behavior began to raise suspicions with the Smith family, and she compounded it by telling them that she "did not want to be deposed in a civil or criminal suit," Bree claimed. "I thought that was a strange statement to make. Why wouldn't she want to testify, to help bring to justice the people who murdered my brother?"

The widening rift between the Smiths and Jennifer became unspannable, and the Smiths cut off contact with her.

But the Smiths continued to question Royal Caribbean's lack of response. The family faced a critical choice. They had discovered that the cruise industry was an unregulated, $35 billion-a-year monolith and that no one had ever successfully fought them in court. Even the FBI hadn't achieved a single successful prosecution in the nearly forty-year history of the modern day cruise industry, which was represented by its lobbying arm, the ICCL. Other families who lost a loved one on a cruise ship usually settled with the cruise line and tried to move on with their lives, often too devastated to fight.

But the Smiths aren't like most families.

From the crucible of their grief, they emerged stronger than ever, with the will to fight a David-and-Goliath battle that would change the entire cruise industry. Bree, the brilliant Columbia law school graduate, resigned her lucrative job in Hong Kong to fight for her brother's cause; Maureen transformed herself from a PTA mom into a passionate crusader for cruise ship safety reform; and George III used every resource at his command to uncover the truth.

For the cruise industry, the perfect storm was brewing.

They decided to hit Royal Caribbean where it hurt—the pocketbook. The Smiths sued for invasion of privacy and intentional infliction of emotional distress. Despite their differences, they also agreed to work with Jennifer, the administrator of George's estate, on her wrongful death lawsuit against the cruise line. As administrator, Jennifer also had to act on behalf of George and Maureen. They wanted the wrongful death action to lead to a court case where they could depose witnesses and get the information they believed Royal Caribbean was withholding.

They also found a powerful ally in Representative Shays, who agreed to hold hearings looking into the cruise industry.

They decided to announce their lawsuit at a press conference just before the hearings, at which they would speak out for the first time since George went missing.

But the cruise industry wasn't going to take it lying down.

———

Connecticut's fourth congressional district, where the Smiths live, has been a fertile breeding ground for politicians of independent spirit for many years. Prescott Bush, grandfather of former President George W. Bush, took a bold and unpopular stance in the U.S. Senate in the 1950s by voting to censure Sen. Joseph McCarthy for his anticommunist witch hunt. Greenwich was home to Sen. Lowell Weicker, the first Republican to blow the whistle on the Watergate cover-up. Ned Lamont, running on a platform opposing the invasion of Iraq, bucked state party brass and won a primary against incumbent Sen. Joe Lieberman in 2006 but lost when Lieberman ran as an independent during the general election.

Shays, an affable, white-haired, maverick Republican, represented the Smiths' fourth congressional district before the November 2008 election swept him and many other Republicans out of office. Despite his party affiliation, Shays was pro-choice and pro–gun control, known for his moderate politics. The George Smith case made him take a closer look at the cruise industry, and he saw a self-regulated industry of foreign-flagged ships with an apparent lack of security. The legal rights of cruise crime victims, along with evidence, dissolved into the murky waters of international law. Shays decided to investigate, even though he knew the cruise industry had a powerful lobby.

"As we began to look into cruise ship safety," he said, "it became clear very quickly that the cruise industry is self-regulated and they have an incentive to cover up and understate any problems." Troubled by his findings, Shays decided, as chairman of the House Subcommittee on National Security, Emerging Threats, and International Relations, to hold congressional hearings on the issue.

"The first step to making cruises safer is to improve reporting of crimes involving Americans onboard cruise ships, ensure these ships have the capacity to properly investigate a criminal activity, and make the information available to the public and cruise passengers," he said.

The cruise industry, which spends millions on federal lobbying each year and thousands on congressional campaign contributions, was not pleased with his plan. "I was encouraged by the industry not to hold my hearing," said Shays, with characteristic understatement.

But this pressure to drop the investigation added more fuel to his resolve. Like the Smiths, he refused to back down. "It merely motivated me to conduct our investigation and hearings with more vigor. I am an idealist, but I also have no illusions, and I can be quite determined when I need to be," he said.

# 7

# FINDING A VOICE

The weather had turned sharply colder, light snow flurries lacing the sky. It was the morning of December 11, 2005, and Maureen, George, and Bree woke up early to get ready for their press conference. After five months of silence, they planned to speak publicly about George's murder for the first time. They were also going to announce their lawsuit against Royal Caribbean and then fly to Washington, D.C., for the congressional hearings on cruise ship safety the next day.

They knew the odds were against them—taking on the mammoth, well-connected, and unregulated industry—but they had to do it. For George's sake.

Maureen knew their efforts would reignite the media firestorm, but they were desperate. They were about to lose every last trace of privacy as the floodgates broke open, but that was the price to be paid for answers. She hoped the lawsuit and its surrounding publicity would shed light on the many unanswered questions about George's murder.

The FBI was investigating, but the Smiths were convinced that the slow pace was due to Royal Caribbean's continued cover-up efforts.

"We had nothing left to lose, since they had already taken everything from us," said George III.

"My son was gone and the individuals who knew what happened to him were involved in a grand conspiracy," Maureen said. "All that I knew and loved about my son was in front of my eyes, and I was not going to let flashbulbs [or] media-hungry news outlets intimidate me in any way. We wanted the word out there, and the media was our tool."

A lack of closure had prevented any sense of healing for the Smiths, and the rupture caused by George's disappearance continued to turn their lives upside down. Bree had quit her job to fight for her brother's cause and had moved back in with her parents. She was also in the process of getting a divorce and attempting to raise her baby as a single mother. For Maureen and George, just getting through every day was a challenge. Some days, the heartsick George III was unable to work at his store.

Christmas was approaching, and tasteful white candles appeared in the windows of the Greenwich colonials in the Smiths' neighborhood. The Smiths dreaded their first Christmas without George, and they knew that the publicity attracted by their lawsuit would force them to relive his murder over and over.

Jennifer would not be joining them at the press conference. She had returned to her parents' home in Cromwell, unable to work as a teacher because of the publicity and upheaval of George's murder. But she was about to hold her own press conference and then launch a public relations blitz that included hiring a Manhattan PR expert, Mike Paul, and appearing on *Oprah* and *Good Morning America*.

The Smiths were unaware of what lay ahead as they pinned the buttons of George onto their dark winter coats and headed to Hartford, driving on I-91 along the Connecticut River.

As they walked up the marble steps of the gold-domed Victorian Gothic capitol building, they were whipped by cold gusts of wind. The family stuck close together, as always drawing strength from one another.

Inside one of the legislative sessions rooms, members of the national press corps jostled for position, setting up television lights and microphones. Despite the Smiths' silence, the case of the missing honeymooner continued to consume the media, especially in the tabloids and on cable news shows.

The Smiths had drawn a tight circle around themselves and their friends and family, but it was about to break. Their lawyer, Brett Rivkind, a fifty-year-old Miami maritime specialist, had been fighting a quixotic battle against the cruise lines in obscurity for years. He had watched the unregulated growth of the industry with alarm, as ships bearing millions of American passengers sailed under flags of convenience with minimal security and without the protections of U.S. laws.

As cruise ticket sales had risen, so had the number of shipboard crimes, according to Rivkind, and he was disturbed by the industry's pattern of "cover-ups and lack of accountability." Off the record, FBI agents had told him that "it was very difficult for them to get cooperation from the cruise lines, and the FBI was frustrated by the difficulty in identifying the number of incidents aboard the cruise ships," he said.

Since the cruise lines reported crimes on a voluntary basis only, Rivkind believed the actual crime statistics were much higher than they claimed, especially sexual assaults. His fight in his native Miami, where the industry had its headquarters, had led to Rivkind and his family being ostracized from some social circles—but like the Smiths, Rivkind was on a crusade.

He had seen horrific cases over the years in which the victims' names were routinely muddied to obscure the crime and to protect the cruise lines' public image. But he believed the industry had sunk to a new low in their conduct surrounding the George Smith case with its massive cover-up and cruel treatment of the Smith family.

Rivkind was hoping that the high publicity focused on the case could serve as a turning point for reforming the industry.

As the klieg lights burned and cameras flashed, the family entered the chambers, grief etched on their faces. Rivkind approached the microphone, and the room stilled.

"The Smith family believes their son was murdered aboard *Brilliance of the Seas* and that Royal Caribbean has deliberately attempted to cover up what happened to George, and to portray this to the media and the public as some sort of unfortunate accident," he said. He cited Royal Caribbean's repeated attempts in the media to portray George Smith's murder as accidental to "protect their public image."

Toward this end, Royal Caribbean "deliberately and intentionally withheld crucial information," he said. The goal of the Smiths' civil suit against Royal Caribbean for invasion of privacy and intentional infliction of emotional distress was to obtain this information and answers for the grieving family. "You don't have to be Sherlock Holmes to deduce that a crime happened in that cabin," Rivkind said.

He accused Royal Caribbean of "negligent security" on the night George went missing. Despite the calls to ship security personnel by neighboring passengers, Rivkind said, "The security personnel never entered the cabin that morning despite being told by a passenger next door that 'all hell was breaking loose in there.'"

The conduct of Royal Caribbean was part of a pattern, he said. "This is a pattern of conduct existing within the company, and anytime there is criminal activity aboard one of their ships, they intentionally downplay the incident and keep it quiet," he said. "The cruise line intentionally pursues a course of investigation and action that interferes with authorities determining the truth and obtaining any convictions of any individuals who have committed criminal activity."

As an example, Rivkind pointed to Royal Caribbean's Miami-based risk management department, which immediately sent defense attorneys to the ship, still in Turkey, after George went missing.

"Passengers reported that the attorneys questioning them were not being objective and were trying to tailor the statements in a way that would protect the cruise line," Rivkind said. He also mentioned the witness accounts of the now-famous bloodstain being "cleaned and removed."

Then Bree spoke. Pale but poised, she gathered force as she progressed, providing a glimpse of her formidable strength as advocate for her brother's cause and cruise industry reform. She spoke of her love for her brother, of his extraordinary spirit and humor, and of the loss that had shaken their lives. "It is inconceivable that he will never again make us laugh, as only he could, on a daily basis," she said.

She lashed out at Royal Caribbean's "lack of response" to the reportedly violent commotion in her brother's room, saying, "If only Royal Caribbean's so-called security force was less negligent, my brother would still be here today." She described the cruise line's treatment of her family as "callous and frustrating," their refusal to provide any answers leaving them with a painful lack of closure.

"Five months after his murder, we have no answers, no body to bury, no grave to pray over," she said. Her words echoed in the high-ceilinged room.

When Bree was done, Rivkind returned to the podium to take questions. A reporter from a major New York City radio station went first.

"Where is Jennifer?" he asked. Several other reporters echoed variations of the question: "Why didn't she come to the press conference?" "Is there a rift?"

The Smith family had just announced that a cruise line had covered up a murder to save its own image, and the first question on the media's lips was about the whereabouts of the pretty young widow.

Rivkind replied that Jennifer was grieving with her own family in Cromwell.

"What should we read into this?" one reporter asked.

"Read nothing into it," Rivkind snapped.

Then Mark Davis, a television reporter from WTNH in New Haven, Connecticut, asked George and Maureen to speak. "We would like to hear from you," he said.

If Maureen felt any sense of hesitation, she didn't show it. The suburban mother who had never taken any kind of stand as an activist or stood in the limelight before stepped up to the microphone. Like Bree, her heartache was visible—but so was her fortitude.

She echoed Bree's indictment of Royal Caribbean's handling of her son's murder and expressed a determination to seek justice. "My son left on his honeymoon and never came home. Something drastic went on aboard that ship that night, and we have to find out what happened," she vowed.

Then George III picked up the baton, continuing the momentum, stricken but keeping his composure. He focused on Royal Caribbean's "bungling of the investigation. When that ship came to Turkey, that ship should have been locked down; it was the crime scene," he said. "Royal Caribbean pulled out of there with the murderers still on the ship."

Unlike families whose grief closes around them like a fist, the Smiths opened their shattered lives to the national press. The small, conservative New England family of three was transforming into one of the most powerful opponents the cruise industry had ever faced. That press conference, the first of several, launched a series of damaging broadsides at the cruise industry and sent it scrambling to regroup.

———

Jennifer broke her own silence almost immediately after the Smiths' press conference. She told the Associated Press that her "dream honeymoon trip had turned into a nightmare." She also launched a website, www.HagelSmith.com, which offered a $100,000 reward for information about George's disappearance. It read:

> *My beloved husband, George Allen Smith IV, disappeared on July 5, 2005, during our honeymoon cruise aboard* Brilliance of the Seas, *operated by Royal Caribbean Cruises. The cruise line reported that George's disappearance was an accident, and it insinuated to the public that it was his fault. We subsequently learned that there is substantial evidence of foul play, including blood in and outside of our cabin and other significant forensic evidence, much of which was quickly destroyed or altered by the cruise line.*

There is also evidence that other passengers and cruise line employees arrived at and/or entered our cabin around the time of George's death.

The Federal Bureau of Investigation (FBI) and the United States Department of Justice (DOJ) for the district of Connecticut have concluded that these circumstances warrant a thorough investigation into my husband's death. My family and George's family have, of course, fully cooperated with these investigations, which the FBI and the DOJ have acknowledged. The joint statement of U.S. Attorney Kevin J. O'Connor and FBI Special Agent Michael J. Wolf can be viewed here.

To date, the FBI and the DOJ have not stated that the cruise line has fully cooperated in the investigation. We are dedicated to finding out the truth about what happened to George and seeing that justice is served. To date, the cruise line has not provided us with the passenger and crew manifest, witness statements taken by the cruise line and its lawyers, videotapes, and many other items and other information, despite our many requests.

Under these circumstances, we are appealing to the American public to help our family. We are offering a REWARD for new information directly leading to the arrest and conviction of the individual or individuals responsible for George's death. Details can be obtained by e-mail at tips@hagelsmith.com or by calling us toll free at 1-800-256-1518 or 305-995-5300.

> *We also ask that you print out a reward poster and*
> *send it to anyone who may have been on the cruise ship,*
> *and post the poster at any of the cruise ship's ports of call.*
> *The cruise ship is now sailing from Miami, Florida,*
> *to the following ports: Oranjestad, Aruba; Cristobal*
> *Pier, Panama; Puerto Limon, Costa Rica; Georgetown,*
> *Grand Cayman; and Willemstad, Curacao. If you live*
> *in or are traveling to one of these ports, please post a*
> *flyer in the local shops and hand them out for us. If you*
> *know of any circumstances surrounding my husband's*
> *disappearance, please help us!*

Later, Jennifer quietly deleted any reference to foul play
on this site, when she herself seemed to be floating a possible
accident theory. (The site has since been taken down.)

At the time, however, Jennifer was advancing the foul-
play theory. In her prepared statement to the press and her
congressional testimony, she said, "I have come to learn that the
cruise line knew all along that there was blood in and outside
of our cabin as well as other substantial evidence of foul play.
As if this were not bad enough, you can imagine my shock
and disbelief when I read a local Connecticut newspaper in
which Michael Crye, president of the International Council
of Cruise Lines (ICCL), blamed George's death on both of
us by stating, 'It's difficult if someone chooses to do harm to
themselves or their companion.'"

She continued: "I don't know if Mr. Crye is married or
if he has children of his own, but I find his reckless remarks

offending our reputations and character both hurtful and irresponsible. I have tried to put these malicious comments in proper perspective, coming as they do from a cruise line, which obviously did not care for the well-being of me or my husband. I see now that it was only our business they valued—not our safety and security."

She said she had also discovered "that Royal Caribbean is a corporate felon involving crimes of dishonesty. They are incapable of protecting U.S. citizens without direct federal oversight and regulation. No other families should have to endure our pain or have their lives destroyed just like the families here today. The cruise industry should spend less time attacking victims and more time making passenger safety its number-one priority."

Jennifer and the Smiths headed to the hearings in Washington.

# *8*

# ANOTHER ALLY

Ken Carver was also on his way to the hearings. A slender, white-haired sixty-nine-year-old, Carver had lived in Darien, Connecticut, not far from Greenwich, for most of his life. He had commuted to New York City to work as president and CEO of the National Life Insurance Company.

Carver retired in 1994 and moved with Carol, his wife of forty-five years, to the affluent Paradise Valley section of Phoenix, with its sprawling stucco castles. Here Carver was enjoying his retirement, pursuing his hobbies in the perennial sunshine of the desert Southwest. On September 1, 2004, Ken and Carol received a phone call with chilling parallels to the one the Smiths received from John Hagel.

The Carvers' thirteen-year-old granddaughter was on the phone from England, anxious and afraid. "Do you know where my mommy is? I've been trying to call her, and she hasn't called back for days. Is she with you?" she asked.

Carver attempted to calm the girl. "Don't worry, we'll call her," he said. "We'll find out where she is."

His granddaughter talked to his daughter at least once a day since divorce had left mother and daughter living on opposite sides of the Atlantic Ocean. After the phone call, Carver had a disturbing sense of foreboding about the fate of Merrian, the eldest of his four daughters, who lived in Cambridge, Massachusetts.

Carver started making calls, but he ran into the same roadblocks the Smiths found. It took him several weeks just to trace Merrian to the cruise ship, since Royal Caribbean hadn't contacted either the FBI or her family when she vanished, he said. Some twenty-six days after she disappeared, Royal Caribbean finally admitted to Carver that she had been on the cruise.

Carver hired a private investigator, Tim Schmolder, the first of a professional team that grew to include several lawyers and other private detectives. Merrian, he pieced together, had flown from Boston to Seattle for a cruise to Alaska on a Mercury ship, a subsidiary of Royal Caribbean, and had vanished at sea.

Carver met with cruise officials for a tour of the ship and described Royal Caribbean Cruises Manager Katy Kzicivan as "initially defensive." She limited his time onboard and refused to name the cabin steward in charge of Merrian's room during her cruise. Kzicivan also refused to let Schmolder interview the security officer in charge of video surveillance. Schmolder was told that videos were erased every two or three weeks and that there was no review of the videos concerning Merrian.

Like the Smiths, the Carvers refused to accept the lack of information without a fight. They hired lawyers in Massachusetts and Florida, where Royal Caribbean is based, and obtained court-ordered subpoenas for crewmembers. In January, two Royal Caribbean employees testified in a telephone deposition that cruise members were aware, even concerned, about Merrian's absence. Yet they did nothing about it, Carver said.

Cabin Steward Domingo Monteiro said he met Merrian on the first day of the cruise and noticed she was missing two days later. "I told my supervisor that this lady didn't sleep in the room," he recalled in a telephone deposition in January 2005, according to a report in the *Arizona Republic*. "He say, 'Do your job.' That's it. He didn't say anything else." Monteiro continued to report her missing for five days.

The last time Monteiro had seen Merrian was on the second night of the cruise, when he brought her two sandwiches from room service. He also said she did not appear sad, upset, angry, or in any way out of sorts.

On the last day of the cruise, Monteiro said he asked his supervisor what to do with Merrian's clothes and belongings. The supervisor told him to pack them up and store them in a locker. Crewmembers boxed up her belongings, disposing of everything but her purse at the end of the cruise. Officials gave her purse to Carver, he told the *Greenwich Citizen*.

"The rest they gave to charity," Carver said, choking back sobs.

Carver pleaded with Royal Caribbean for help. Eventually the head of the risk management department called to say that the Carvers would get the information requested in their subpoenas. In the documents they learned that, contrary to their initial statements, ship officials had reviewed the videos related to Merrian's disappearance.

In March 2005 the Carver family gathered at the United Methodist Church in Paradise Valley for a remembrance ceremony for Merrian. They refused to call it a memorial service.

During the ceremony, Carol was praying with eyes closed. She still believed Merrian would knock at their door any day. The Carvers' granddaughter was motherless at thirteen, alternately in a state of shock and pure anguish. Through his grief, Ken felt a growing rage, fueling his determination to fight. He decided to sue.

Through the spring and summer, the Carvers and their lawyers requested documents from Royal Caribbean, but the cruise line didn't respond. Carver fell into a routine, spending his day calling and sending e-mails to the police, the Coast Guard, and the FBI, trying to keep the search for his daughter alive. His office, once filled with tranquil photographs of desert mountains and sunsets, had become command central in his search for answers, filled with growing files of court documents, notes, and newspaper clippings.

In August the Carvers filed suit against Royal Caribbean for damages in a Miami court. When reporters questioned the cruise line about the suit and Merrian's disappearance, the company issued a statement that stunned the Carvers. Royal Caribbean declared Merrian dead—despite a lack of evidence and a private investigator's report that didn't rule out foul play, Carver said.

"Ms. Carver had severe emotional problems, had attempted suicide before, and appears to have committed suicide on our ship," said the October statement. "The death of Merrian Carver is a horrible tragedy, but, regrettably, there is very little a cruise line, a resort, or a hotel can do to prevent someone from committing suicide."

"Do they have information that we do not have?" Carver asked. "If there is a video of her jumping overboard, I would think they'd want us to see it. This was just their way of trashing Merrian," he said, breaking down. "So why would they try to cover it up if it was supposed to be a suicide? That does not make sense."

He couldn't accept this conclusion with no evidence, and the way the cruise line stonewalled his requests for information again raised his suspicions. "Why did they cover up her disappearance?" he asked.

Despite a crack team of lawyers and private detectives, Carver's battle left him and his wife feeling lonely and frustrated. Then he saw a show on CNN about the George Smith case, which was attracting a large media spotlight. A reporter on the show mentioned Representative Shays's congressional hearings. Struck by the similarities between the two alleged cover-ups, Carver went to Washington.

"Merrian will return," Carol told him as he was leaving.

He knew she wouldn't, but he was going to fight for answers to honor her memory in any way he could. "I couldn't walk away from it," he said. "I couldn't take a pass on it. They had the wrong guy."

# 9

# Scandal Management

On the night before the hearings, Richard Fain, Royal Caribbean's CEO, worked deep into the night at the company's six-story headquarters looming over Miami Bay. Palm trees ringed the massive building, and the pole bearing the company's flag drummed against the halyard in the breeze.

The cruise line had come a long way since 1968, when it launched its one-ship operation on a shoestring budget, working out of a trailer on the outskirts of town. It now employed forty-four thousand people on approximately twenty megaships and ended 2005 with a record profit of $716 million, on which the company paid no federal income tax.

Fain had enjoyed a remarkably successful career with Royal Caribbean. He ranked fourth on the *Forbes* list of highest paid CEOs for 2004–05, receiving a salary of nearly $1 million and a $2.12 million bonus. The value he realized on option shares was $8.5 million—not surprising, given the 58.31 percent total stock return for 2004. That year Royal Caribbean Cruise also gave him $17,992 worth of "membership dues, discounts on company cruises, and expenses for spousal travel" for him and his wife, Colleen.

Fain, his wife, and their four children lived a luxurious life in southern Florida among the gated stucco mansions with their tiki huts, marble decks, and waterfalls in gardens filled with citrus trees, orchids, and bougainvillea. But Fain was facing one of the worst crises of his career with the George Smith scandal and the congressional hearing. The Smith case had caused a public relations debacle of a magnitude that Fain had never seen in his twenty years with the cruise line.

Also working with Fain that night was Adam Goldstein, Royal Caribbean's president since 2005. The forty-eight-year-old Goldstein had a degree from Princeton, a law degree from Harvard, and a salary of nearly $2.75 million, which afforded him and his wife, Cheryl, and their two children the same luxurious life in Miami-Dade County that Fain and his family enjoyed.

They both fit the image of "Ivy League nerds," as their arch rival Carnival Cruise Lines liked to say. In turn, they referred to Carnival as the "Kmart of the Seas." It was galling to Fain that Royal Caribbean and its classy image had become fodder for the tabloids with the Smith case.

Royal Caribbean had faced damaging publicity in the past with other passenger disappearances, sexual assaults, and norovirus outbreaks. There also had been a felony conviction for environmental dumping during the Clinton presidency. But none of those episodes came close to generating the spectacular publicity of the George Smith case: a young couple with matinee idol looks on their tragic honeymoon cruise splashed across every possible media outlet.

Congress had tried unsuccessfully to regulate the cruise industry before, but the spectacle of the public hearings with the grief-stricken Smith family was something entirely new. The cruise industry had always managed to sail under the radar, and the deregulation policies of the Reagan-Bush years had helped them do it.

But they had never been in such a glaring media spotlight before, and the FBI was taking an active role in the investigation of the George Smith case. In New Haven, U.S. Attorney Kevin O'Connor, speaking for the FBI, described the Smith case as "suspicious" and called for an "aggressive and thorough" investigation. Another FBI spokesman said it was "the most active case and highest priority case" in the state.

However, the cruise industry had an ace up their sleeve with their powerful congressional lobby. Their lobbying arm, the ICCL, had deep pockets, spending $2.9 million in congressional lobbying from January 2004 to July 2005, according to the Center for Responsive Politics. That's nearly $1 million more than Wal-Mart spent during the same period.

Despite the problem with Shays, the Royal Caribbean executives knew they had friends on his committee, especially Congressman John Mica, a Florida Republican. According to OpenSecrets.org, Mica received $3,000 in campaign contributions from Carnival for his 2005–06 campaign. He also received $1,000 from Fain, and Fain had donated the same amount for Mica's 2002 and 2004 campaigns. Mica also received $11,000 in contributions from the sea transport industry—companies involved in the shipping of goods over bodies of water, both domestically and internationally.

Mica's Republican colleague from Tennessee, John Duncan, received $12,797 from the sea transport industry during the same period. Fain hoped they could depend on those two congressmen at least.

Fain should have been reveling in his achievements after all his years at Royal Caribbean's helm. He had presided over explosive growth for the company, which now boasted twenty-one ships and two under construction, including the most grandiose of all, *Genesis of the Seas*—an unprecedented, 220,000 ton, 5,400-passenger project featuring a replica of New York's Central Park with live foliage and park-view balconies. The model for the supership sat on Fain's desk, complete with skyscrapers inspired by those surrounding the Manhattan landmark.

Instead of basking in his accomplishments, Fain was trying to contain the damage of the Smith case, which was taking its toll on company stock. The value of the stock continued to tank in inverse proportion to the level of publicity, dropping 8.5 percent in just seven days in January 2006, the week that Jennifer appeared on *Oprah*, according to the Safe Cruise blog.

The cruise industry was suffering one of its first major setbacks in the nearly forty-year history of the modern cruise industry. As stock shares of Royal Caribbean and Carnival both declined, business analysts such as Robert LaFleur of the Susquehanna Financial Group cited the negative publicity surrounding "guest disappearances at sea, fires" and other "events," according to the *South Florida Sun Sentinel* in August 2006. "Each new event compounds the growing public image that something is amiss in the cruise business," LaFleur wrote in a report for investors. However, LaFleur's report also cited "rising fuel prices," and experts also attributed "softening demand" for cruises and vacation travel in general, as the economic downturn later began to take its toll.

Fain knew the publicity was about to get worse—much worse. The night before, the Smiths had appeared on the *Joe Scarborough Show* from their home in Greenwich. Sitting together on their couch, their body language underscored their tight-knit bond. They also struck all the right notes with the audience—sympathy for their grief and admiration for their determination.

They were extremely compelling: the heartbroken father, the feisty Irish mother who wasn't going to rest until she found out what happened to her son, and the young Columbia-trained lawyer who was fearless when it came to seeking justice for her brother.

On the show, Bree described her brother as "happy and contented, with a new wife and promising career in front of him." Maureen said her son was "kind, polite, and loyal, with a wonderful sense of humor." Scarborough asked if he got the humor from her, with her Irish background, and Maureen laughed, offering a glimpse of the happy family they had been before the tragedy. George III had difficulty containing his emotions and said they would never be the same. "We have been out of our minds with grief. We were robbed."

All three painted a picture of Royal Caribbean as callous and unresponsive. Not only had they refused to provide any information about George's disappearance, they had never even extended their sympathy. "They've been working overtime to protect their image," George said. "I hope Congress takes action for the other murders and rapes on cruises."

"Royal Caribbean wants George's disappearance to be a tragic accident," Bree added. "But the FBI has a lot of good information, and they are not going to let it go."

Then Maureen said something that particularly rankled Fain: "It is time to speak out so Congress makes changes and other families [do] not have to suffer. There is a sinister underworld to the cruise industry."

*A sinister underworld!* This hardly fit their carefully crafted "Love Boat" image.

The show ended with Scarborough expressing his outrage about the tragedy that had struck "these wonderful people" because of the lack of security and transparency on cruise lines. He said he hoped Congress would address the need for "reforming the industry."

Fain knew this was just the beginning. He could imagine every talk and cable news show salivating to get the Smiths and Jennifer now that they had broken their silence. With each new television appearance, the stock value would drop.

, Jennifer also appeared on *Scarborough*, right after the Smiths, but as he watched the show, Fain began to see a light on the horizon. Jennifer didn't appear to be a typical grieving young widow, like Fain had imagined. Unlike the Smiths, Jennifer didn't seem visibly distraught. She sat through the interview strangely stone-faced and didn't shed a tear. Dressed in a sleek black pants suit, with a new hair style and impeccable makeup, she appeared to have had a makeover—not typically a priority for a heartbroken young widow.

Jennifer also made claims about her treatment by Royal Caribbean after George went missing, saying she was "kicked off the ship" and left to fend for herself in Kuşadasi. Fain believed her statements were not completely true, and he seized on them as ammunition. He thought he could refute them, at least in part, since Marie Breheret, Royal Caribbean's guest relations manager; a representative from the American consulate; and a vacationing FBI agent had accompanied Jennifer during her stay in Kuşadasi after she left the ship. This could be the centerpiece of Royal Caribbean's game plan and a highlight of the website they would launch: The Top Ten Myths Regarding Royal Caribbean's Handling of the Disappearance of George Smith.

Royal Caribbean officials believed that Breheret had been with Jennifer from the time she was taken from the spa to her questioning at the Turkish police station. Breheret had also accompanied her when she went to a hotel that night, which they believed was arranged by Royal Caribbean. They also claimed that Jennifer was allowed to make any calls she wanted after George went missing, despite Jennifer's claim that she was not allowed to call the Smiths. This is also listed on their "Myths" website.

The cruise line also claimed that "reports that she was forced to wear clothing with the company's logo are false," the website says. "Mrs. Hagel Smith requested a change of clothes, since she was still in the clothes from the night before. Breheret helped her get a change of clothes before leaving the ship to be interviewed. At approximately 11:35 a.m., one and a half hours after she had been located in the spa . . . Mrs. Hagel Smith was taken to a private room and offered an opportunity to shower, rest, and change clothes before her interview with Turkish authorities. Mrs. Hagel Smith accepted. Because her cabin was sealed, Mrs. Hagel Smith had no clean clothes. Breheret therefore asked staff to get comfortable new clothes from the ship's gift shop, which typically carry the cruise line insignia."

Royal Caribbean hired Lanny Davis, the scandal management Washington lawyer known for representing Bill Clinton in the Monica Lewinsky case. They also dispatched Capt. Bill Wright, a Royal Caribbean senior vice president who wore a white uniform and looked like *The Love Boat* captain, to represent the cruise line at hearings and get ready for a round of talk shows. Wright would be accompanied by Crye, the hulking former Coast Guard captain and president of the ICCL.

The spotlight was an uncomfortable place for Royal Caribbean and the cruise industry. They preferred to keep a low profile, with their foreign-flagged ships operating out of U.S. ports. Under this arrangement, the cruise lines, enjoy the benefits and protections provided to U.S. companies but bear few, if any, of the responsibilities. Foreign-flagged ships are not only exempt from federal taxes but also from following various federal laws.

By contrast, a U.S.–flagged ship must be crewed by U.S. citizens, pay taxes, and is subject to U.S. law. Crimes or incidents onboard, no matter where they occur, must be reported to and investigated by U.S. authorities and settled in U.S. courts. Carnival, for example—headquartered in Miami but incorporated in Panama—noted that their public records boast "that substantially all of our income in fiscal 2004, 2003, and 2002 . . . is exempt from U.S. federal income taxes," according to an article in the *Washington Post*. Most cruise ships are registered in countries such as Liberia, Panama, or the Bahamas, where regulations concerning crimes are less strictly enforced—if at all.

# 10

# The Industry

Before the increasing speed, safety, and affordability of airplanes made them the preferred method of intercontinental travel, the best—and often only—way to get to your overseas destination was by boat. There were enormous ocean liners, yes, but the cruise industry didn't exist as an organized group then because a boat was the only way to go. That changed over the course of the twentieth century—starting in 1903 with the Wright brothers in Kitty Hawk, North Carolina; continuing with advances in aviation technology during World War I; and culminating in the aviation industry largely as we know it today after further developments during World War II.

The modern cruise industry began in the 1950s, when Miami shipping magnate Frank Fraser launched the *Nuevo Dominicano*, flagged in the Dominican Republic. The new concept was small cabins. Ship designers historically had built staterooms as large as possible to accommodate passengers during long ocean crossings. Ed Stephan, a former hotel worker who became one of the founders of the cruise industry, devised a new plan for smaller cabins to allow for more passengers on larger ships.

The Fraser family joined forces with Israeli businessmen Meyer Halevy and Ted Arison, the latter founding Carnival Cruise Lines, which made him one of the world's wealthiest men. Arison passed the business to his son, Micky, a college dropout who favored tinted sunglasses and shirts unbuttoned down his chest—unlike Fain and the other Royal Caribbean executives in their dark, conservative suits and ties. Following Fain on the list of top-earning CEOs, Micky Arison had a salary of $700,000 and a bonus of $2.4 million. As owner of the Miami Heat basketball team, among other investments, Arison's overall worth was estimated at $5.3 billion.

Royal Caribbean is owned by octogenarian Sam Ofer, an Israeli shipping tycoon reportedly worth $3.1 billion. Ofer began his career as a delivery boy for a shipping company and manages his business from Monte Carlo.

*The Love Boat* television show, which debuted in 1977, played a major role in the industry's boom. The show took place on Princess Cruises' *Pacific Princess*, and guest stars included Mickey Rooney, Jamie Lee Curtis, Janet Jackson, and Michael J. Fox, with much emphasis on romantic entanglements. Capitalizing on this lighthearted image, the industry launched its first national television campaign with commercials showing Kathie Lee Johnson (later Gifford) singing and dancing on a "fun ship cruise."

Over the years, this "fun" extended to include pole wrestling and beer chugging contests as the industry's image slid from straitlaced to increasingly informal. On Royal Caribbean's *Freedom of the Seas*, so-called "groove cruises" began sailing in October 2004. Lingerie-clad passengers danced to "sensuous vocals and dirty bass pumping from the speakers, Vodka Red Bulls and glow sticks in hand," according to the *New York Times*. "As long as you're not barefoot in the dining room, you're pretty much all right," Ted Arison said.

When *The Love Boat* and the Kathie Lee commercials premiered, an estimated 825,000 cruise passengers were sailing out of North American ports. A decade later that number had spiked to nearly three million passengers. But crewmembers usually don't describe their vessels as "fun ships." Flags of convenience allow cruise lines to hire crew from mostly Third World countries, without mandatory background checks. The wages are low and the working conditions difficult.

Many crewmembers take the jobs to escape the desperate conditions of developing countries. They work as maids, waiters, and maintenance and kitchen staff, sometimes logging fourteen-hour days without a day off for as long as ten months at a time. The lives of these workers are rigidly structured, paramilitary style, according to Bob Dickinson, Carnival's president, in *Selling the Sea: An Inside Look at the Cruise Industry*. "If they do not perform their duties in a prescribed manner, they are subject to discipline," he said.

The faux naval uniforms of the captain and other ranking officers visually suggest the military and the captain's absolute authority over the crew.

In *Cruise Ship Blues: The Underside of the Cruise Industry*, Ross Klein, a professor at the School of Social Work at Memorial University in Newfoundland, described the life of a crew worker.

> *While the working conditions for officers, cruise staff, and those working in the shops and casinos are adequate, if not good, the experience of those working in the dining room, cleaning rooms, in the galley, and below deck is quite different. These workers are often paid substandard wages, have marginal accommodations, survive on inadequate food, and live under a system that is rife with abuse and uncertainty.*
>
> *[Most of the untrained workers come from] under-industrialized countries in Asia, Eastern Europe, the Caribbean, and Central America. They are seduced by the idea of getting paid to travel the world on some of the most modern and beautiful ships.*

As the International Transport Federation (ITF), representing seafaring workers, confirms, "Below decks on virtually all cruise ships, there is a hidden world of long hours, low pay, insecurity, and exploitation. Those who work continuously below deck, like in the galleys or ship kitchens, rarely see the light of day, let alone the shimmering sea of the Caribbean."

Crewmembers may work fourteen hours a day, seven days a week, and earn less than $400 a month. The most overworked may be the shipboard waiters, who may work as many as sixteen hours a day and often get less than six hours of sleep a night. Often there is no health insurance or other benefits, and crew are housed in overcrowded quarters and work dangerous jobs without proper safety equipment. Complaints can lead to incarceration, fines, or deportation, according to Klein.

Because of the foreign flags governing the ships, the laws concerning the crew's labor rights are vague and lax at best. The Center for Seafarers' Rights said that Bahamian-flagged vessels have no laws governing the number of hours a seaman may work or how many days off he or she must receive. Liberian maritime rules do not guarantee "a right to shore," and Panamanian laws only state that wages must not be "remarkably unfair" in relation to the average wage in the industry.

Because of the working conditions caused by the flags-of-convenience system, the ITF recently launched a campaign to help crewmembers on cruise ships. "The owners of most cruise vessels take full advantage of the . . . lack of employment rights," the ITF says on its website. Discipline for crew members is "harsh and randomly applied," and "the industry has been riddled with episodes of sexual harassment at sea."

One of the ITF's goals is an end to the flag-of-convenience open-registry system. But cruise industry officials counter that they provide opportunities for thousands of poor workers to improve their lives. "They are coming for economic opportunities. Nobody puts a gun to their head," said Ruthano Devlin, spokeswoman for Miami-based Tropicana Cruises, according to an article in the *Sun Sentinel.* "We all do the same thing," added Tim Gallagher, spokesman for Carnival.

Crewmembers who have attempted to improve their working conditions have faced severe repercussions. In 1981, 240 Central American workers went on strike aboard a Carnival ship in Miami to protest the firings of two coworkers. Carnival promptly called the U.S. Immigration and Naturalization Service, which declared the strikers illegal immigrants and flew them home. The threat of deportation looms over the heads of all cruise ships workers who complain, according to Klein.

"They treat crewmen like an orange," said Charles Lipcon, a Miami attorney who represents more than one hundred crewmen annually. "They squeeze and squeeze, and when there is nothing left, they throw away the peel."

Sexual exploitation is another disturbing reality of crewmembers' lives. Victims of sexual assaults fear stepping forward because doing so jeopardizes their jobs, Klein says. Victims are both male and female and may be forced to perform sexual favors in return for keeping their jobs or as a condition for promotions.

As the cruise industry boomed in the '70s and '80s, Washington lawmakers attempted to address the flag-of-convenience system a few times—with little success. When Bill Clinton was elected president, he tried to crack down on foreign corporations that didn't pay taxes in the United States as a means to finance his health care and education initiatives. But his effort stalled, thanks in part to the cruise industry's powerful lobby.

Clinton's administration also gave a fresh head of steam to a bill by Missouri congressman William Clay that required that the Fair Labor Standards Act and the National Labor Relations Act apply to most foreign-flagged ships using U.S. ports. The bill would have forced cruise ships to abide by U.S. minimum-wage standards, collective bargaining rules, and other legal protections for crewmembers.

"We have heard of mariners being required to work eighteen to twenty hours a day for less than $1 an hour, of living conditions so unsanitary they threaten life . . . of sailors abandoned in foreign ports and blackballed for seeking to improve conditions that all would agree are intolerable and inhuman," Clay said. He also claimed that his bill could provide thousands of jobs to U.S. citizens.

The bill was reintroduced to Congress in 1993, and the cruise industry blasted it. In his criticism, Fain cited Ronald Reagan's theory of overregulation and overtaxation of business by government. Overseas, the United Kingdom, the European Union, and Japan also condemned the measure. If passed, the bill would mean a loss of around $1 billion in goods and services that cruise lines or their customers purchase in Florida annually, said Arthur Kane, of the Florida Caribbean Cruise Association.

The bill died in Congress.

But the Clinton presidency offered more trouble for the cruise industry in the form of independent and indomitable Attorney General Janet Reno. She obtained a felony conviction against Royal Caribbean for dumping waste oil and hazardous materials overboard, often at night, off the coast of Puerto Rico. The cruise line paid $8 million in fines. "Royal Caribbean used our nation's waters as its dumping ground, even as it promoted itself as an environmentally 'green company.' This case will sound like a foghorn throughout the entire maritime industry," Reno said.

Both Carnival and Royal Caribbean have histories of environmental violations. Investigations by the *Miami Herald, New York Times,* and CBS News revealed that from 1993 to 1998, cruise ships were involved in eighty-seven cases of illegal discharges of oil, garbage, and hazardous wastes into U.S. waters and have paid more than $30 million in fines.

In April 2002 Carnival Corporation pleaded guilty to falsifying records to cover up pollution by six ships over several years, according to Klein. A lawsuit followed, filed by Bluewater Network, the Environmental Law Foundation, San Diego Baykeeper, and Surfrider Foundation against Carnival, Princess Cruise Lines, Royal Caribbean, Holland America, and others for illegal discharge of ballast water into shoreline waters. Ballast water is carried in the bottom of ships for stability and often contains residual oil. The cruise lines agreed to pay $75,000 to research alternative ballast water management technologies and settled the suit.

The ICCL responded with what would be become their standard response to negative publicity: voluntary guidelines. No law was enacted, despite Reno's urgent call for reform, as the industry slipped through the regulatory cracks once again.

While governor of Florida, Jeb Bush, closely allied with the cruise industry, was roundly criticized for his role in pushing a $236 million federal contract for Carnival Cruise Lines to house Hurricane Katrina victims.

The cruise industry also faced negative publicity with a series of shipboard outbreaks of norovirus, a particularly virulent and highly contagious illness with symptoms that include diarrhea, stomach cramps, and projectile vomiting. Cruise ships provide a fertile breeding ground for the illness in part because of the close living quarters of so many people, according to the Centers for Disease Control and Prevention (CDC).

In 2006, notes Klein, the number of cruises with illness outbreaks increased 59 percent and the number of sick passengers and crewmembers in those incidents rose 62 percent compared with figures from the previous year. In one outbreak in January 2006 aboard the *Queen Elizabeth 2*, almost one in five of the ship's 1,600 passengers fell ill.

According to the CDC, outbreaks on cruise ships are usually traced to contaminated food or water or to viruses brought aboard from shore, either before the cruise or at a port of call or from person-to-person contact with a sick person. The only way to prevent the spread of the sickness is to disinfect the ship and quarantine those who are ill.

But Michael Sheehan, spokesman for Royal Caribbean, claimed it was the passengers not the crew who could be the source of the problem. Sheehan said crewmembers are monitored heavily on the ships.

*It is the guests who are boarding and disembarking on a weekly basis that make the issue more difficult. We discuss outbreaks with the CDC on a given sailing, and we go through a series of possible similarities on where the illness may have begun. If someone's a waiter, for example, and they're servicing ten tables at an early seating, you track the guests. You can pinpoint where the virus starts. The crewmembers are not causing the outbreaks.*

The norovirus outbreak created unpleasant headlines for the industry, with newspapers such as *Newsday* calling the *QE2* the "Good Ship Kaopectate" in 1987, when fifty passengers and crew became ill with the virus.

But that episode paled in comparison to what the industry faced with the George Smith case on the eve of the Shays hearings, as they launched into full damage-control mode.

# 11

# Strength in Numbers

On the morning of the Shays hearings, a small group gathered in Shays's office in the Rayburn House Office Building in Washington, D.C. The Smiths and Ken Carver were joined by two others who also had stories to tell.

Son Michael Pham, a Vietnamese refugee, wore a crisp white shirt and a blue tie. His parents, Hue Pham and Hue Tran, had disappeared while on their dream vacation aboard a Carnival Caribbean cruise in May 2004. Like the rest of the group, he was holding a picture of his missing family members. It was the last photograph ever taken of his parents. On the cruise, both are wearing glasses and short-sleeved vacation shirts. An exuberant Mr. Pham has his arm wrapped around his wife, who is smiling shyly. The story had many striking parallels to both the George Smith and Merrian Carver cases. Shays listened and took notes.

The Pham family came from Saigon. After the city fell at the end of the Vietnam War, Hue Pham strapped his baby daughter onto his back and fled with his wife, Son Michael, and another son, a disabled polio survivor. In Saigon harbor, they jumped onto a container ship. They drifted in the choppy waters of the South China Sea without food and water for two weeks until the U.S. Air Force spotted and rescued them.

The Air Force brought the family to a fugitive camp in the United States, from which they settled in Westminster, California, in Orange County—known as Little Saigon because it has the largest population of Vietnamese Americans in the United States. Here the Phams became citizens, got blue-collar jobs, and worked hard.

"My dad had to repair railroad tracks by hand on his knees, and my mom worked in an assembly plant, but none of that mattered because we were finally free," said Son Michael in an interview with the *Greenwich Citizen*. "Why would the sea save my parents only to take their lives thirty years later?"

The couple raised five children and had just retired. They were pursuing their hobbies: cooking, gardening, and playing cards. They also cared for Hue Tran's elderly father, who lived in a nearby nursing home.

For Mother's Day in 2005 their children bought them the first vacation of their lives, a seven-day Caribbean cruise on the Carnival ship *Destiny* between Barbados and Aruba. The brochures showed decks awash in people soaking up the sun and sipping umbrella-laden cocktails or dancing on deck to a live reggae band, surrounded by the aquamarine Caribbean

Sea. Accompanying them would be their daughter Sharon and her daughter, one of the couple's nine grandchildren.

After the cruise, the Phams planned another trip. In November they were going with Son to return to Vietnam for the first time in thirty years to visit relatives they hadn't seen since Saigon had fallen. They were looking forward to this "unfinished life business" with great anticipation, Son Michael said.

The Phams, Sharon, and her daughter boarded the *Destiny* in San Juan, Puerto Rico, on May 9, 2005. Registered in the Bahamas, the palatial ship, with its nine-story open atrium and glass elevators and three Olympic-size swimming pools, defied the imagination of the retirees. As they sailed toward Aruba, the couple ate dinner in the two-story dining room. Afterward, the Phams decided to go to a show.

Just before midnight, the telephone rang in the cabin that the four family members were sharing. It was the reception desk, asking Sharon to come and retrieve something. At the desk, a steward handed her a plastic bag containing her parents' flip-flops and her mother's purse, found on the deck where her parents liked to sit.

Alarmed, Sharon looked for her parents but couldn't find them. Neither could the crew. But Son Michael said it took almost three hours after the Phams' disappearance before the first announcement went out over the ship loudspeakers. The crew waited another four hours before notifying the Coast Guard, as the ship sailed farther away from the spot where the Phams had vanished.

The deck where his parents' flip-flops were found wasn't sealed off until several days later, when the FBI met the ship in St. Maarten. Not one passenger was questioned, and the ship continued on its journey, Son Michael said. "They were more focused on planning the next day's shore activities in St. Maarten than protecting crucial information and evidence pertaining to their two missing passengers."

Carnival suggested that his parents may have committed suicide, just as Royal Caribbean had with Merrian Carver's disappearance. Carnival officials said that the Phams' sandals and other effects on a deck chair indicated suicide. Son Michael emphatically rejected that conclusion, saying his parents were having a wonderful time with their daughter and granddaughter and were looking forward to their upcoming trip back to Vietnam.

"Two American citizens with no personal or financial problems, no serious health problems, living the happiest time of their lives, both vanished without a trace or witness," he said.

Son Michael flew to his parents' home in California but found no clues suggesting they had taken their own lives. The FBI had ruled out suicide, but the agent in charge of the case did mention an employee who had made racial comments about his parents while he was investigating, Son Michael said. He wanted to "be careful not to speculate."

Like the Smiths and the Carvers, Son Michael said he received no help from the cruise line, which, he said, failed to provide any answers and covered up his parents' disappearance, and then compounded the tragedy by hinting it was suicide.

"Carnival refused our requests for assistance and failed to provide us with any information," he said. "They had an arrogant business-as-usual attitude."

As Shays began to see the deepening implications, the group exchanged hugs and words of empathy with Son Michael.

---

"I know the pain, sorrow, and emptiness of not understanding why your son is not coming home from what was supposed to be a wonderful, safe vacation," said Jean Scavone, a reserved, dark-haired high school guidance counselor from Meriden, Connecticut. She shared a tragic connection with the Smiths. Her son James had vanished from a Carnival cruise ship exactly six years, to the day, before George Smith went missing, and James had vanished from the same ship as the Phams: the *Destiny*.

James, a George Clooney lookalike, had been a scholar-athlete, excelling in tennis and soccer, and had just graduated from Western Connecticut State University. He was accepted into New York University's prestigious graduate program in city planning, which he would start that fall.

According to Scavone in an interview with the *Greenwich Citizen*, Carnival had floated a suicide theory about James, telling passengers that a broken engagement had probably caused James to commit suicide. "This is a total fabrication," Scavone said. "Absolutely untrue."

Scavone believes that violence played a role in James's disappearance because a passenger later told her that on the morning of July 5, 1999, the phone rang in her cabin and she heard a young man say, "Help me, I can't get out of here."

"She heard a scream, furniture being thrown around, and scuffling. Then the phone went dead." There were also ear-witness accounts of the noise, another parallel to the George Smith case. Scavone said the ear-witness was told by Carnival's corporate office "that they had no record of anyone disappearing from the ship. It's as if they had no record that my son ever existed."

When Scavone tried to contact Carnival officials about her son's disappearance, they refused to take her calls. "It's so unreal and so horrible," she said. "There is no closure when your child has died and you don't know why or how."

———

Shays had also received written testimony from Rita Sittig, whose son, Christopher Caldwell, had gone missing from a 2004 Carnival Mexican cruise. Sittig said Carnival never informed her of Christopher's disappearance. Instead she found out from her daughter that the Coast Guard had called off the search for his body.

"Those words were like a bomb going off in my head," she wrote on the International Cruise Victims (ICV) website.

"All I could do was scream and cry. That day, a part of my heart was destroyed and can never be replaced. I still look at his pictures with his three girls, and I can't believe that he is really gone from us."

Sittig raised the issue of the lack of security on the ships. "If . . . there had been video surveillance cameras monitoring the deck where he had last been seen, maybe he would be here today. Perhaps we wouldn't have been forced to go through such intense grief."

Sittig said that Carnival did only a "slight search" to find Christopher and were "no help at all" to her family when they were trying to find answers. "I am unable to even watch a Carnival Cruise advertisement on TV without crying," she wrote.

———

As the group compared notes, they believed they saw a pattern. By refusing to provide any answers or assistance, the cruise lines had deepened and compounded the families' tragedies in order to protect their public image with standard risk-management protocol. The family members noticed striking parallels in the way the cruise lines handled the loss of their loved ones, the subsequent alleged cover-ups, and attempts to portray disappearances as accidents or suicide.

"All of us had lost loved ones from cruise ships, and all had no answers and the same story: no witnesses, no surveillance tapes, no motive, and no help from the cruise company," Son Michael observed.

The group put on their winter coats and walked across the street to the congressional building, carrying the pictures of their missing family members. They were quiet as they entered the imposing Capitol Rotunda, bracing for a fight. They made an unlikely group of grassroots activists. None had any experience with any kind of activism, social or political. Because of his independent spirit, Shays had barely survived his last election. He was reportedly on the outs with his own party and about to provoke them further with this inquiry into one of their major campaign donors.

"All we had were our stories," said Carver. "We knew it was going to be an uphill battle." But a formidable force propelled them. "We had passion," said Son Michael. "Our passion comes from our tragedy."

Most of them thought it was a long shot at best.

———

The Smiths sat next to Jennifer at the hearings, all of them wearing the button pictures of George, but the similarities ended there. George III's grief had been like an open wound since he lost his son, and he was wrestling with his emotions as he sat in the chambers, trying not to break down. Jennifer was again stone-faced and dry-eyed. She wore a new, layered hair style and a black suit with a slate-blue shirt unbuttoned slightly to reveal a strand of pearls.

George didn't like having to put on a public show of unity with Jennifer. She was staring straight ahead—coldly, it seemed—with an invisible demarcation line running between them. The Smiths did not speak to Jennifer, and she made no attempt to communicate with them.

Maureen and Bree broke down in tears several times during the session, but the family presented a unified front, supporting and comforting one another. The media circus had followed them to Washington, and a television crew was preparing to film the proceedings. A press table in the corner teemed with reporters from the *New York Times, USA Today,* the Associated Press, and other media outlets.

Some of the media were focusing on George IV's drinking and partying instead of the alleged murder and alleged cover-up by Royal Caribbean. It was mortifying, especially for a family from conservative Greenwich, but the family had decided that they would do whatever it took to get answers. If that meant opening themselves and George IV to this kind of media exposure, so be it.

*What am I doing here?* thought George III. He should have been at home in Greenwich, getting ready for Christmas with the family. It was Bree's baby's first Christmas, and they would have had a wonderful celebration, with the tree in their family room and the smell of Maureen's Christmas cookies baking.

An NBC film crew was setting up lights and microphones. Next to Maureen sat Brett Rivkind, then Ken Carver, Son Michael Pham, and Jean Scavone. Before the hearings began,

Capt. Bill Wright, Royal Caribbean senior vice president, sat down on Maureen's other side, although there were several other empty seats in the chamber. George stared at him, but Wright fixed his gaze straight ahead at the congressional panel as the proceedings were about to begin.

"Isn't there any other place to sit, Bill?" Rivkind asked Wright, gesturing toward the vacant seats. "Why are you sitting here?"

Without speaking, Wright stood up and moved.

Widely ranging ideologies separated the congressmen on the panel, from liberal Democrats Dennis Kucinich and Bernie Sanders on one end of the spectrum to conservative Republicans John Mica and John Duncan on the other. Shays, the moderate, tried to bridge the gap. He began by raising his concerns about possible negligent security and criminal activity onboard cruise ships. Because of the way cruise vacations are marketed, "people think they should have no fear on them," he said.

"Cruise passengers can be blinded to the very real perils of the sea by ship operators unwilling to interrupt the party for security warnings," Shays continued. "And after an incident occurs, a thorough investigation can be profoundly difficult when the crime scene literally floats away, on schedule, to its next port of call." For the unregulated cruise industry, "There has never been any oversight—ever."

Shays noted that the members of the Smith family "await justice and ask that no more families endure avoidable tragedies. . . . We hear their call for safer seas and are absolutely determined to pursue the investigation of George Smith's disappearance, and we look for greater candor, accountability, and responsiveness from those entrusted to carry precious cargo into a vast, inherently hazardous realm."

Then Shays read testimony from the Smiths, who charged Royal Caribbean with a comprehensive cover-up of their son's disappearance. They pleaded passionately for cruise ship safety reform, saying, "Heavy lobbying by the cruise industry has resulted in placing passengers at risk on cruise ships and leaving passengers and their families with little or no rights. The time has come to stand up to the cruise industry and protect American citizens by passing new laws that make the cruise industry accountable for passenger safety and preservation of crime scenes, strengthen passenger rights and law enforcement's powers."

Attached to the statement released to the press was a photograph of a radiantly handsome George Smith in Mykonos. "Please don't let George die in vain. We end this statement with great sadness but hope for the future that changes will be made to protect innocent passengers, like our beloved son and brother, who sail on cruise ships."

George III let out a sob when Shays finished. Maureen and Bree were crying too. Shays frowned, seeming increasingly upset. There was still no reaction from Jennifer.

"Is a cruise the perfect place to commit a crime?" Shays asked passionately. The room buzzed, as did the panel, surprised by the change in the normally understated Shays.

Then Shays read Jennifer's testimony, which again blasted Royal Caribbean and the cruise industry for portraying George's disappearance as an accident, despite her claim that they knew "all along there was blood in and outside our cabin as well as other substantial evidence of foul play."

Her written testimony then moved away from George back to her claim that Royal Caribbean had kicked her off the ship and left her to fend for herself in Turkey after George was murdered. She painted a traveler's nightmare: "I was left in Turkey with no money, no plane ticket, no food, nothing. . . . The cruise line did not offer to help with a flight, hotel arrangements, or anything. I could not speak the native language, and I felt abandoned," Shays read.

"This sends a shiver down my back," he said. "When you read Jennifer's statement, you want to scream."

Then cruise industry officials, including ICCL president Michael Crye, gave testimony that included statistics on cruise crime for the first time ever. He said that of the twenty million passengers who took cruises from 2003 to 2005, thirteen people went missing and there were 178 reports of rape and sexual assaults.

But Shays questioned the statistics, since cruise ships are not required to report crimes. "We are citing statistics that I think are meaningless," he said. "I'm wrestling with how can we trust any statistic from a cruise line that could do what they did to a young wife."

Crye said that after the Turkish police completed their investigation of the ship on the day George Smith went missing, they told the captain he could clean the blood off the overhang at 6:00 p.m., and by 7:00 p.m. they allowed the vessel to sail out of Kuşadasi. The FBI had not yet boarded the ship. "There were no commercial decisions involved," Crye said.

Shays asked why the blood was cleaned before the FBI could conduct their forensics investigation. Turkish police "saying you can doesn't mean you have to," he noted.

Crye replied that ship officials were in contact with the FBI and would have cooperated with any of their requests if they had been asked to do so. "If the FBI had chosen to go aboard that ship that day and exercise their jurisdiction, the cruise line would be more than accommodating."

Two admirals from the Coast Guard and one from the Navy also said they could not be confident about statistics reported voluntarily. Rep. Elijah Cummings, a Democrat from Maryland, called the industry policy of voluntary reporting of crimes "a major problem." But Congressmen John Mica and John Duncan defended the cruise lines, as Fain and Goldstein had hoped. Mica commended the cruise industry for devising an affordable vacation for the middle class.

Gregory Purdy, director of safety, security, and environment for Royal Caribbean, claimed that the company had handled the incident "correctly and responsibly" and had followed the proper protocols. "Royal Caribbean promptly notified the FBI, the American embassy, the Turkish police, the Greek Coast Guard, and the Bahamas

Maritime Authority about Mr. Smith's case," he said. "The Smith family has suffered a tragic loss. We extend our deepest sympathies to the family. We do not know what happened to George Smith—only that he tragically disappeared from the cruise—but we continue to cooperate fully with the FBI in the hope that the agency will be able to provide solid answers and some measure of closure for the Smith family."

Carver, Scavone, and Son Michael also told their stories, struggling with their emotions as they attempted to get through them. At the end of Son Michael's testimony, he described how his parents were looking forward to returning to Vietnam. Instead they disappeared from the cruise under mysterious and suspicious circumstances. "They always wanted me and my brothers and sister to do the right things, to help others," he said. "I hope, by sharing our story with all of you, it is the right thing to do. . . . I trust that all of us here today can work toward better protecting the traveling public."

"The timing is really good," Rivkind said in his statement about his twenty-two years battling cruise industry cover-ups. "In all the time I've been doing this, this is the most attention that I've seen. This is the turning point, maybe, in the history of the cruise line industry."

———

Afterward, Shays told the group that he would push for an additional hearing in March if they could compile a list of at least ten families who had been victimized on cruise ships. "No more families should have to endure avoidable tragedies," he said. Cummings backed him up. "There is a major problem," he said again. "We cannot allow this to continue the way it is because there is going to be another incident, whether we like it or not."

The Smiths invited Carver, Scavone, and Son Michael to join them at their news conference. Thrust into the spotlight, the quiet New England family was leveraging all the publicity they could to battle a billion-dollar industry. They saw how media coverage could translate into a sharp focus on the need for cruise ship reforms and spare other families from similar tragedies.

With Carver, Scavone, and Son Michael, they decided to form a cruise victims' advocacy group and launch a website. They called it International Cruise Victims (ICV), a nonprofit fighting for legislative reform to protect passengers from crimes and provide support to victims of cruise crimes and their families. The nonprofit had no money, just a handful of volunteers, but ICV soon became a powerful international force with members in twenty countries, inspiring growing numbers of cruise crime victims to step forward to join the growing call for reforms.

"I couldn't change the industry, the Smiths couldn't change the industry, but as a group, we could," said Carver.

The perfect storm was gaining momentum, and it was about to wash over the cruise industry, indelibly changing the landscape. But the industry wasn't going down without a fight.

## 12

# STORMY WATERS

The morning after the Shays hearings, Fain was up early, angrily flipping through a stack of newspapers on his desk. The headlines all sounded about the same: The *New York Times*, "Taking on Crime aboard Cruise Ships"; *USA Today*, "Cruise Safety in Spotlight"; and the AP, "Disappearance of American Man Spurs U.S. Probe of Cruise Ship Safety."

The AP story appeared with a photo of the tight-faced Crye flanked by a distraught Maureen and stone-faced Jennifer, both wearing their button photos of George. The AP story ran in almost every major newspaper throughout the country. It began: "The disappearance of an American man during a honeymoon cruise is drawing congressional attention to a seamy side of the glitzy sea cruise industry."

Fain was also most likely hearing early reports about a stock slide caused by the coverage. It was only the beginning. *Time* magazine was planning a cover story, "Crime Rocks the Boat," and had asked Fain for a comment.

The Smiths and Jennifer were preparing for a barrage of talk shows, including *Good Morning America*, *Oprah*, *The Today Show*, *48 Hours*, *Larry King*, *Nancy Grace*, and *The Abrams Report*, among many others. The story of the "missing groom" had riveted the American public, and the network and cable shows began a nightly duel for the latest pieces of information.

Carver was doing his own media blitz, breaking down every time he tried to talk about how Royal Caribbean gave his daughter's belongings away to charity. News of the formation of ICV was inspiring more victims of cruise crimes to step forward almost daily. To Fain, it was a nightmare.

"We are in a media firestorm," said James Walker, Jennifer's maritime attorney, with glee.

But Fain and the cruise industry had beaten back nearly every challenge before, and they had vast financial resources. Royal Caribbean created a battery of press releases, including one that defended protocol on the ship after George went missing:

> *We enabled the investigation to take place by notifying all the relevant authorities immediately. They came onboard and they did their forensics while the cabin was sealed, while the bloodstain was sealed down below. They did the forensics, and they were in constant consultation with the FBI. The U.S. consulate was there . . . All of the relevant authorities were involved in determining how the investigation should be carried out.*

Lynn Martenstein later added that the Turkish police conducted a full forensics investigation. "They took samples. They took photographs. They dusted for fingerprints. They did their forensic investigation of both the cabin and the overhang. They spent the better part of the day on the ship." She also said that Royal Caribbean turned over ninety-seven of the ship's video surveillance tapes to the FBI.

Then Royal Caribbean launched the website, The Top Ten Myths Regarding Royal Caribbean's Handling of the Disappearance of George Smith, in response to "a lot of inaccurate and unfair speculation about our company's response to the incident."

Highlights included the "myth" that Jennifer had been kicked off the ship without assistance or support, as she had claimed before the Shays committee. The site refuted her claim, saying that Jennifer had been given a choice of remaining on the ship, in another cabin, but she chose to leave. The site also claimed that she was not abandoned but was accompanied by Marie Breheret, the vacationing FBI agent, and someone from the consulate. Breheret had arranged Jennifer's hotel, and they had taken her to the airport the next day, according to Royal Caribbean.

Another "myth" was the charge of a cover-up, which included destruction of forensic evidence, such as the blood on the canopy below the Smith cabin. Instead Royal Caribbean said that they notified the FBI immediately after they learned George was missing, and the Turkish police conducted a proper investigation "in liaison with the FBI."

Also, Captain Lachtaridis had only ordered the blood washed off the balcony at 6:15 p.m., with permission from the Turkish police, for the safety of guests "who were hanging far over the railing to take photographs." Royal Caribbean insisted the cabin was sealed and no evidence destroyed.

It was also a "myth" that crewmembers saw a bloody trail or signs of a struggle when they took Jennifer back to her cabin that morning. Reports of a violent confrontation in the Smith cabin also made the list of myths because only complaints about "partying noises" and "drinking games" were heard.

The penultimate myth was perhaps the most problematic: "Cruise ships are unsafe." In response, Royal Caribbean posted:

*According to FBI statistics, the incident rate of violent crime in the U.S. is 465.5 per 100,000 inhabitants. Last year, the cruise industry carried over 10 million guests and employed over 120,000 crewmembers. On average, from 2000 to 2005, approximately 50 crimes against U.S. citizens were reported to the FBI each year. This equates to approximately one crime per 200,000 cruise passengers last year . . . More than seven million guests sailed on Royal Caribbean ships during the last two years. During that time period, the company had five man-overboard incidents, which include the George Smith incident. Of those five incidents, the one involving Mr. Smith is the only one where there was any suspicion of foul play."*

Once the website launched, Fain dispatched Capt. Bill Wright and Capt. Michael Lachtaridis to appear on the talk show circuit with the Smiths. He also told Lanny Davis, their heavyweight scandal-management lawyer, to get ready to step into the ring for a few rounds.

Lachtaridis appeared on MSNBC's *The Abrams Report* on January 5 alongside Maureen, and it backfired royally. Maureen struck a sympathetic chord with viewers, emerging from the nightmare of George's murder with heartbreak written on her face but filled with composure and determination.

Lachtaridis infamously had encouraged passengers to enjoy the sunset the night after George's disappearance, calling it "an issue we hope to resolve shortly." On *The Abrams Report*, he began with a clumsy attempt to put forward the accident theory. He surmised that the heavily intoxicated George had wanted to smoke a cigar or "get some fresh air from the balcony. He was sitting on the railing and lost his balance."

Certain members of the press, including Bryan Burroughs in a *Vanity Fair* article, accepted this as the likely reason for George's death, despite all the evidence to the contrary. Former FBI agent Greg McCrary had said that when crewmembers brought the incapacitated Jennifer back to the room, both the door to the balcony and the curtains to that door were closed. Why would George close both the curtains and the door if he were sitting on the deck?

Abrams questioned Lachtaridis about the blood in the room, which suggested foul play. "That's the only question," Lachtaridis responded understatedly.

Maureen strongly objected to the smoking accident theory: "This is Royal Caribbean's common approach, to blame the victim, whether dead or alive, to detract attention from their wrongdoing, their cover-up, and we're not letting this go because something really bad happened to my son on a Royal Caribbean ship."

Abrams then asked Lachtaridis if there was a cover-up, if "the captain and Royal Caribbean wanted to just put this behind them as quickly as possible, including washing the blood off the canopy later that day?"

"When they complete the investigation," Lachtaridis replied, "I asked the police before they leave the ship, 'Can we secure now the cabin, can we clean the blood?' They said, 'Oh, yes. It's clear now.'"

Abrams wondered why Royal Caribbean didn't lock down the ship and stay in Turkey due to "an obligation to say, 'You know what, one of our passengers is missing, and as a result it's probably better for us not to just continue with the cruise.'"

"To do what in Turkey?" the captain asked. "To wait there? For what?"

Then Lachtaridis claimed that ship officials asked Turkish authorities to "come aboard and they refused." But Jerry Askin's videotape clearly contradicted this statement. Lachtaridis also denied Jennifer's claims, as described by Abrams, that she was left in the middle of a country that she knew nothing about, with no money, no clothes, and no help. Appearing confident for the first time in the interview,

Lachtaridis said, "No, this is a lie. This is a lie. Why she's lying, I don't know."

Also on the show, Susan Filan, a former Connecticut prosecutor and MSNBC legal analyst, had strong words for Captain Lachtaridis's accidental death theory: "What happened was you've got a captain who pretty much said, 'Hey, man overboard, accident.' But what it really looks like now is it's very likely a crime scene, a homicide that was mishandled. It's a cover-up. It's gone badly, and now they're coming out, all guns blazing."

MSNBC's website hyped the show with a headline that said, "Captain's Comments Stir Up Smith Case." Instead of defusing the controversy, he had stoked it. Soon after this appearance, Captain Lachtaridis took an early retirement from his position at Royal Caribbean. The cruise line denied that his retirement had any connection to the George Smith case. Cruise officials reportedly started asking not to be placed on television shows opposite the tenacious Maureen.

Vito Colucci Jr., a high-profile private investigator and former Stamford police detective, was also commenting on several of the shows devoted to the story. He told the *Greenwich Citizen* that he was convinced it was a homicide. "I have believed from the start that it's a murder case," he said. "All the evidence shows that foul play was involved; for example, the 'ear-witness' accounts of the arguing in Smith's cabin before he disappeared, the loud thud that was heard. And the FBI would not be spending all this time and money investigating the case if they thought it was an accident."

The Smiths later hired Colucci to help with their investigation. "I only take cases I believe in, and I believe in the George Smith case wholeheartedly," he said.

When asked if he thought the FBI would obtain their first-ever cruise crime conviction with the case, Colucci said, "I have the highest respect for the New Haven FBI because they helped keep me alive when I was with the Stamford PD. I have a lot of respect for them."

On December 13, 2005, *Dateline NBC* updated its report about the case, hosted by reporter Dennis Murphy. The show included the ear-witnesses from adjacent cabins, who elaborated on their accounts.

Clete Hyman, the deputy police chief, described what had jolted him out of his sleep that morning: "A little after four o'clock in the morning, we were awakened by what I'd call loud cheering, something like a college drinking game. This happened two distinct times." Hyman, a thirty-one-year police veteran well-versed in homicide investigations, instinctively checked the time and called security to complain. He banged on the wall, but there was no response.

"The voices continued," he said. "They weren't as loud as they were during the drinking games. But then after a couple of minutes, we heard voices outside the door of the Smith cabin. I don't recall hearing the door open. I assumed they were leaving the party. But that was just my impression at the time."

The tone soon changed, though. "Then we heard what sounded like arguing out on the balcony. . . . It wasn't a physical confrontation. It was just like they were arguing over some type of point."

Next Hyman said he heard someone say "good night," and he heard the cabin door open and voices receding in the hallway. "So I waited for a couple of seconds and then opened the door and looked out."

"What did you see?" Murphy asked.

"I saw three younger males walking down the hallway. Young males—but only three of them—leaving George's cabin." Then Hyman said he heard what sounded like furniture moving. "My impression was, 'Good! They're cleaning up the room.'"

As it approached 4:20 a.m., "[The noise] appeared to be concentrated out on the balcony area. The chairs on the balcony are metal, so they make a different type of sound. I heard that noise, and then there was silence. It got very quiet. Heard no voice. It was just very quiet." About three minutes later, he heard a horrific thud.

"The first thought in my mind was somebody fell on the balcony, because it was the last place I had heard anyone. However, I quickly dismissed that because the noise was just too loud. There was actually a reverberation to the noise. And somebody just falling, you know, off their feet to something on a balcony would not cause that much noise."

Greg and Pat Lawyer, on the other side of the Smith cabin, also awoke to the commotion that night on nearly the same timeline. They didn't hear sounds of a drinking game, but they did hear furniture being moved, Greg said. "All of a sudden there was a lot of noise coming from the cabin next door, and what it sounded to me like is somebody was throwing things against the wall, like throwing furniture in the room against the wall or against the floor."

"'What in the world is he doing there?'" Pat kept asking, "and I did use the term 'he.' I didn't use the term 'they' because we did not hear any voices."

Next came "maybe a series of shuffles and bangs against the wall, and then it ended with one big thud like somebody had picked up the couch or the sofa and thrown it against the wall. And then that occurred, it was maybe a stretch of like two minutes, something like that, where these thuds took place, what I call trashing the room, and then it went quiet." After the loud thud, both Hyman and the Lawyers heard someone knocking on the Smith cabin door at approximately 4:30 a.m.

Greg Lawyer opened his door and saw two uniformed ship personnel standing outside the Smith cabin. "And I looked at them and said, 'Hey, you guys better get in there because that room is trashed.' That's exactly what I said, and then they sort of gave me the 'hi' sign. They didn't say anything."

The cruise line confirmed they were ship's security officers responding to the noise complaint Hyman made just after 4:00 a.m., but because the cabin was now silent, Royal Caribbean said the uniformed men left without entering.

Also appearing on the show was Josh Askin's lawyer, Keith Greer, who described a dramatically different scene at 4:00 a.m. and also offered some striking insights into the events of the night.

In the casino that night, bad luck had plagued Jennifer, Greer said. "George at one point in time went over to the table with Jennifer, and she had been losing, not big, but losing—and he had to go back to the room and get some money to come back and give it to her."

After the casino closed at 2:30 a.m., Greer said that the Smiths, Askin, Kofman, and the Rozenbergs took the elevator to the disco bar on Deck 13. Also in the elevator was the casino manager, presumably Botha. Askin witnessed the casino manager flirt with Jennifer in front of George.

"Jennifer's there on the other side of the elevator with the casino manager next to her with his arm around her in the elevator . . . And at that point Josh recalls looking at the other boys in the elevator because it was awkward," Greer said. "The way that the touching, the holding—it just didn't seem right."

"So presumably, George is seeing the same kind of thing taking place?" Murphy asked.

"Yeah, but everybody's still happy. Everybody's still jovial," Greer replied.

According to Greer and Josh's version of events, the tension escalated at the disco, when Josh saw the casino manager and Jennifer continue to flirt. "Jennifer's there, but there's a couch adjacent to the table. Jennifer sits down on the couch with the casino manager sitting right next to her."

Other witnesses, including Margarita Chaves and Dominick Mazza, saw George and Jennifer exchange words and Jennifer kick him in the groin. Askin didn't see the kick but saw Jennifer leave with the casino manager. Then George and his companions drank shots of absinthe until around 3:30 a.m., when the bartender closed the lounge.

"The lights go on," Greer said. "Time for everybody to go to their rooms. The Russian boys and Josh escort George back to his room."

"Does George get there under his own power?" Murphy asked.

"No," Greer said. "By that time, George was dropping his cigarette, according to Josh. He was about 50 percent on his own power on the way back to the room. He wasn't being carried, but he was being guided with some assistance of the two larger boys."

"Where's Jennifer?" Murphy asked.

"That's the big question," Greer replied.

When George found his cabin empty, the group went looking for Jennifer, according to Greer, searching near the Jacuzzi in the solarium. Not finding her, they went with George back to his cabin, but here Josh's version of events diverged markedly from Hyman's and the Lawyers'.

According to Greer, Josh used George's bathroom as the Russians put George to bed. "The other boys put him down on the bed, take his shoes off, leave the room. 'Goodbye

goodbye, let's go, we're outta here.' They go down to one of the Russian boys' rooms, order an incredible amount of room service, room service shows up 4:30, 4:45 with the food. They eat. Josh is back in bed by 5:15 that morning."

When Jennifer and the four men were questioned by the Turkish police in the ship's lobby the next morning, one thing struck Josh particularly. "The biggest thing was she's wearing the same dress she was wearing the night before. She's distraught . . . There's a question of 'Where's George?' And Jennifer says to Josh: 'What happened? I blacked out. I don't remember anything after the casino.'"

"She drank too much and passed out?" Murphy asked.

"Blacked out," Greer replied.

Cliff Van Zandt, an NBC News analyst and former FBI agent and profiler, also appeared on the show. "When you look at this picture here, do you see this point right here?" he said of one of the photos. "That looks like that was pooling blood. This is ten feet-plus wide here, so if a human body fell here, this is perhaps evidence of a head injury."

"A bleeding kind of injury, right?" Murphy asked.

"A bleeding where there was continued bleeding," Van Zandt replied. "It can be blood that had been contaminated with water, sea spray, something like that, which made it spread out like this. Perhaps George Smith, by whatever means, went over the balcony two floors down—he crashes on top of this metal awning. He lays there for a while, he's already bleeding. He bleeds out a little bit. And then he starts to crawl. Does he pick himself up? Does he zig when he should have zagged? Or does someone come upon the body and help it over the side?"

———

The following year, in an appearance on CNN with Paula Zahn, George Smith III made a startling correction to the timeline on the night his son went missing. "What most people don't realize is that ten minutes before Jen was brought back, two Royal Caribbean employees went into George's cabin looking for George," he said. "This has not been out there before. This is a new timeline. And we think that when they went into George's room, they saw the crime scene, and they would have realized that something had gone down."

Walker carried it one step further. "So, if the security guards had simply listened to what the passengers were begging and got in there and taken a look around, they would have found his blood. If they had looked outside, they could have stopped the ship and tried to save him, or looked for him, or they could have perhaps found him on the awning and saved his life."

The cable news shows were trying to outdo one another with new angles on the story almost every night. The Smiths began every talk show with a statement like this one, made by Bree on *The Rita Cosby Show*: "My brother, George, was murdered at the age of twenty-six with a promising future and a lifetime of happiness ahead of him."

Capt. Bill Wright, also on the show, defended Royal Caribbean as having followed proper protocol and urged viewers to visit the myths website.

Cosby seemed skeptical and asked why *Brilliance of the Seas* was not locked down in Kuşadasi after George went missing. "Hindsight's 20/20, but is it possible you let a murderer go free?" she asked Wright. "You let the ship sail."

"There was nothing at that point that indicated a murder," Wright said.

———

As sometimes happens with the press, many of the reports latched onto a single sentence: "The Smith family has claimed their son had been murdered and charged Royal Caribbean with covering it up to protect their public image." Lanny Davis held a conference call with members of the press to defend Royal Caribbean. He admonished reporters for using this language and insisted that he wanted it stopped immediately. Lynn Tuohy, a veteran reporter from the *Hartford Courant,* dressed Davis down for dictating to reporters what language to use when they covered the news.

———

The missteps and gaffes continued for the cruise line. Bob Dickinson, Carnival's president and CEO, described George's disappearance as a "non-event . . . entertainment" at a cruise industry convention in Miami. "I hate to see you talk about it because you're giving it legs," he said to a reporter. "It has nothing to do with safety on cruise ships."

Furious, the Smith family wrote a letter to Carnival's board of directors, asking for an apology and Dickinson's immediate termination. "These statements are despicable," they said. "Bob Dickinson's view that George's murder is a non-event is definitely not shared by George's family and friends. . . . George's murder is not 'entertainment' to those of us who mourn his loss every day." Their letter also pointed out that the FBI and Congress had spent millions investigating George's disappearance and cruise ship safety in general "so that similar 'non-events' do not happen to other cruise ship passengers."

The more the industry tried to deflect attention, the more it fueled the storm. After their appearances at the hearings and on the talk shows, the Smiths noticed suspicious activity— odd and threatening phone calls and e-mails, and cars that followed them. The harassment by unknown persons made the desperate family more determined to fight. "They took everything from us they could possibly take, so we have nothing else to lose," said George III.

The Smiths spent that frigid northeastern winter in a series of television studios. At night when they came home from New York City, they often found George's friends parked in front of their home, holding silent, lonely vigils.

# 13

# In the Vortex

Meanwhile, the scrutiny and criticism of Jennifer continued to mount. She set to work with her publicist, Mike Paul of MGP and Associates, to clean up her image. *Sports Illustrated* had nicknamed Paul "Mr. Fixit" for his counsel of pro athletes in crisis, including New York Jets defensive end Mark Gastineau, who had a highly publicized extramarital affair. Paul began referring to himself and Walker as Team Hagel Smith and launched into "crisis action." He also announced that Jennifer had retained the services of high-profile forensic scientist Dr. Henry Lee, of O. J. Simpson trial fame.

The media spectacle reached its zenith at the end of January 2006, when Lee boarded *Brilliance of the Seas* in Miami to see if he could find evidence of George's murder. Camera crews and photographers jostled to get shots of Lee and his team, dressed in navy-blue jumpsuits, "Forensic Lab" emblazoned in yellow on their backs. Yellow harnesses allowed Lee and his team to hang over the balcony on Deck

9, next to the Smith cabin. He stared down at the overhang that had been covered with the famous bloody stain.

Although Dr. Lee said the FBI had the carpet and other important items from the cabin, he attempted to conduct a belated *CSI Miami*–style investigation. When he emerged from the ship, he said he did find "something of significance."

The Smiths denounced the spectacle as a publicity stunt.

———

Mike Paul also booked appearances for Jennifer on high-profile shows such as *Good Morning America* and *Oprah*. Her image evolved. Gone were the revealing bikinis and low-cut dresses from her honeymoon, replaced by shirts buttoned up to her neck—not even unbuttoned enough to show her pearls. She also shed her stoic demeanor, which had been criticized by the public as cold-hearted.

Weepy and edgy, she appeared on *Good Morning America* with Diane Sawyer. Dressed in a white Oxford shirt and a black pants suit, she looked more like a prim New England principal than the glamorous young bride she had been. She repeated her claim that she had no memory of the night George disappeared. She dismissed Sawyer's questions about her drinking, saying, "Yes, we were drinking. Yes, we were having a good time. We were on our honeymoon. Does that mean that we were two alcoholics and were just crazy and didn't know our limits? No."

Then she bitterly criticized the public, which had shown her little sympathy, and then came the tears that had been missing at her previous public appearances. "Forgive me, America, for not always being what you expected every step of the way," she said. "You expect that when you lose your husband, that you come home and grieve with your family and their arms around you and you get left to your feelings."

Soon after, she made a much longer, highly publicized appearance on *Oprah*, again wearing the buttoned-up white Oxford shirt, this time with a conservative gray pants suit. Again her tears flowed steadily.

The interview began with Gayle King, a former news anchor at WFSB in Connecticut, interviewing Jennifer, who sat stiffly with her hands clasped in her lap. Jennifer insisted that she remembered nothing from the time she and George arrived in the casino in the early morning of July 5.

"That sounds suspicious," King said. "Had you been drinking?"

Jennifer said she had been partying and "celebrating her honeymoon," but not enough to cause a blackout.

King questioned Jennifer about reports that she'd had a nasty argument with George and had kneed him in the groin.

"If that is the last encounter that I had with my husband, then that is something I will have to carry for the rest of my life," Jennifer said, her eyes welling. "I can't remember anything from a certain time period. We just aren't angry people. George would never call me names. And I would never do something like that out of anger to George."

"Why didn't you think there was a problem when you woke up in your cabin without George?" King asked.

"At that point I wasn't the sharpest knife in the drawer," Jennifer said. "I was just found unconscious four hours earlier. I was very groggy." As for her missing husband, she assumed he spent the night in a friend's cabin.

Jennifer's cabin had been trashed, according to ear-witness neighbors. In her attack on Michael Crye's accidental death theory, Jennifer herself had claimed that blood was in the cabin. But on *Oprah* that day she told King that she didn't worry about George's whereabouts until cruise staff approached her at the spa while she was having her massage. So how did Jennifer keep a spa appointment four hours after having been found unconscious in the hallway if she was so groggy, and why did she arrive ninety minutes early?

Jennifer dissolved into tearful defensiveness. "Everybody wants more from me. I want more from me," she said. "Why don't I have more? Why don't I have the answer? I do feel guilty that I'm alive and George is not. I would trade places with him in an instant."

A few moments later, Adam Goldstein, president of Royal Caribbean, took a seat beside Jennifer and made his first public comment on George Smith's murder. Why had he waited six months? Speaking with almost preternatural calm, Goldstein offered his sympathy to Jennifer, then denied any cover-up. Jennifer smiled broadly at him. Goldstein claimed that the Smith cabin was sealed until Turkish authorities completed a forensic investigation but didn't mention that the investigation took all of two hours and didn't include questioning of key witnesses in the case.

Goldstein also denied that Royal Caribbean preemptively cleaned or painted the bloodstain on the awning, saying that it was cleaned after receiving assurances from Turkish authorities that the cruise could continue. He insisted that the investigation had been conducted properly and that they had been in "constant consultation with the FBI."

Jennifer wondered, "Why not leave the ship in Turkey?" she asked. "Why not just keep it there? Why not keep the passengers on? Why not talk to all of them?" But she didn't press the point any further. Instead she focused on her own version of the details, that Royal Caribbean only offered her "CDs, magazines, and a sedative," that she had to spend the day in Kuşadasi waiting for her parents to wire her money for her ticket home. She was softening her previous account of having to fend for herself in a foreign country.

She asked for an apology from Goldstein, who graciously obliged like a running back seizing an easy opening. "Absolutely, we should have paid for your ticket home . . . We did the best we could, that we knew how in a situation that we had not encountered before . . . I am sorry, on behalf of the forty thousand people at Royal Caribbean, that we were not able to render you as much assistance and comfort as you would like to have had on that terrible day," he said.

But how could Goldstein say that Royal Caribbean had never encountered this "situation" before when Crye had testified that thirteen cruise ship passengers had gone missing since 2003, including several on Royal Caribbean ships? At the next set of hearings, industry officials increased that number to twenty-four. If it had happened before, why wasn't Royal Caribbean prepared for this kind of emergency?

The show ended with Jennifer breaking down and describing her regrets, beginning with her increasingly strained relationship with the Smith family. At the last moment, she returned to the loss of her husband. "George was George IV," she said. "There should have been a George V and George VI. Why wasn't I there to protect George? Why wasn't I in that room?"

She finished by saying that the public should realize that the famous missing honeymooner was simply "our George, that we love him so much. This has been just such a nightmare for everybody. Just stop bashing him. Stop saying he was 'this' or 'that.' He was a wonderful person. He was a great husband, even for the short time. For all the years that I've known him, there's not one person who can say a bad word about him."

After the show, Jennifer began meeting secretly with Goldstein and Fain. These backchannel communications took place without Walker. In later testimony, Jennifer claimed she began exchanging e-mails with Goldstein and then meeting with him and Fain in "weird places like airport hangars." There the cruise lines executives expressed their worries about the impact of her wrongful death lawsuit. That the president and CEO of Royal Caribbean were holding clandestine meetings with Jennifer in airport hangars leaves no doubt about the magnitude of their concerns about the case.

---

After Jennifer's appearance on *Oprah,* the blogosphere buzzed with opinions. On Scared Monkeys, a website that offers commentary on current events, politics, and pop culture, appeared posts like "She didn't even cry when talking about it. I would think it would be very traumatic. How could you smile and be so uncaring?" or "I think she had something to do with his death; she has been nothing but evasive since it happened, never a comment or anything, and she seemed to distance herself very rapidly from her new husband's family. I got the impression that his sister never liked her, and frankly, I didn't either."

But Jennifer had her defenders, too, who thought George fell overboard while drunk. This post appeared on the honeymoon cruise murdersteryblogspot, a blog that sprang up in 2006 in response to the case: "I am seriously disturbed by this attitude that if a woman doesn't weep and cry and gnash her teeth on TV for the lurid entertainment of everyone not involved, that she is somehow a liar or a murderer. This is a sad accident. He was drunk, went out on the balcony, and fell over and into the sea. No one to blame . . . Leave the woman alone. No one should have to mourn a loved one and be a performing monkey for the public at the same time."

---

The four young men Jennifer and George had befriended on the cruise also did the cable news circuit. On *The Abrams Report*, Susan Filan and Walter Zalisko joined Dan Abrams for a new show about the missing groom that focused on the Russians and Askin. The show began by running parts of the videotape taken by Askin's father. Abrams and his guests watched the Turkish police tell Askin that Jennifer was going to be arrested for murder and his now well-known emotional defense: "She was with another man . . . the casino manager. You have to get him in here. I'm not letting her go to jail. I'm not letting her go to jail!"

Botha's lawyer, Andrew Rier, stated that "there are ship records to prove that Lloyd did not leave the disco with Jennifer . . . The timeline at 3:20 puts Botha in his room, and the Smiths are still upstairs in the disco along with these Russian gentlemen."

The video shows Askin telling Turkish authorities that "George and Jennifer were very happy, very happy. They were on their honeymoon. He was happiest. He was happy . . . when we left him." But Abrams showed a clip from *The Today Show* in which Greer, Askin's attorney, directly contradicted Josh's depiction of George. Greer said, "It's speculation at this point. We don't—was George upset? You know, his wife was not there. She was missing. He had been drinking all night. Did he injure himself hitting something? Did he cut himself on some broken glass?" Greer also said that the loud commotion Clete Hyman and the Lawyers heard that night was "George at that point in time, dropping furniture and moving furniture."

George Smith III and George Smith IV on a family vacation in Crete in 2002. *(Courtesy of George and Maureen Smith)*

George Smith IV and Jennifer Hagel at their Newport wedding reception on June 25, 2005. *(Courtesy of George and Maureen Smith)*

*Brilliance of the Seas* docked in Miami, Florida, in 2011 with a close-up of cabin 9062 and the metal overhang on which bloody handprints had traced a path over the side of the ship. *(Courtesy of Gerry Hill)*

Ken Carver and Congressman Chris Shays in Shays's office before the December 2005 congressional hearings on cruise ship safety in Washington, D.C. *(Courtesy of Ken Carver)*

George Smith III, left, makes a statement during a December 2005 news conference in Miami with Attorney Brett Rivkind; his daughter, Bree; and wife, Maureen. *(AP Photo/Lynne Sladky)*

George Smith IV's mother, Maureen, left, and widow, Jennifer Hagel Smith, right, listen to the testimony of Michael Crye, center, president of the International Council of Cruise Lines (now the Cruise Lines International Association) at a December 2005 congressional hearing in Washington, D.C. *(AP Photo/Kevin Wolf)*

Capt. Bill Wright, senior vice president of fleet operations of Royal Caribbean International, at a January 2006 news conference in Miami. *(AP Photo/Alan Diaz)*

James Walker, the attorney who had represented Jennifer Hagel Smith in her wrongful death lawsuit against Royal Caribbean, later representing the Smith family, at a January 2006 news conference in Miami. *(AP Photo/Alan Diaz)*

Jennifer Hagel Smith at the March 2006 House Government Reform Subcommittee hearing on international maritime security involving cruise ships on Capitol Hill in Washington, D.C. *(AP Photo/Lauren Victoria Burke)*

Bree Smith and Son Michael Pham in March 2006. Smith and Pham, along with Ken Carver and Jean Scavone (not pictured), cofounded International Cruise Victims to raise awareness about cruise ship safety. *(Courtesy of Ken Carver)*

"These stories simply don't add up, and the lawyer going on record this morning and making these statements that already are consistent with other witness accounts and with what law enforcement is able to piece together so far, I find extremely curious and very interesting," said Filan.

Filan also wondered about Josh's emphasis on ruling out Jennifer, saying, "Doesn't that suggest to you, Dan, that he does have pretty good information about what happened and knows that she isn't involved?"

Zalisko saw a red flag in Josh's repeated insistence on Jennifer's innocence. "There obviously is a problem with the stories and the fact that the one suspect is trying to convince everyone that Mrs. Smith had nothing to do with it. How would he know that? The investigators should be prying a little more into that, and I'm sure that, you know, as a seasoned investigator, he has a lot more information to give us and possibly implicate the two other individuals that were in that room."

Abrams then raised the point that "it could be, on the other hand, that he [Josh] just liked her, right, and he was thinking to himself, you know what, I just don't want the authorities to start looking at this woman, who seemed like a very nice, loving, newly married woman."

———

Rusty Kofman's attorney, Albert Dayan, also made some appearances on cable shows, including *On the Record,* hosted by Greta Van Susteren. He repeated the same details of the story, from his client's perspective, as Josh Askin had relayed. But then he made a startling claim: Rusty Kofman, the young law student, with "cautiousness of innocence" had decided to cooperate with the FBI. "He actually met with the FBI agents on three separate occasions and was grilled," Dayan said. "Of course they were very kind to him at first, but when they did not get a confession to whatever they thought actually had happened on the ship and a confession corroborating foul play, they would get into this young man's face so close that they would actually spit into his face and propound theories of guilt."

The FBI told Rusty "they had witnesses that saw him do it, that they had witnesses that had observed him push Mr. Smith over the balcony. This young man remained astern into the position of innocence," Dayan said.

# 14

# Out of the Box

In the widening spotlight, new cruise crime victims stepped forward almost every day. "Their secrets are out of the box and can never go back in," said Maureen.

In Monterey, California, Marilyn Decker downloaded a picture of George Smith, a man she had never met, and put it in her wallet. It was "to remind me that George and my daughter Jamie and countless other cruise crime victims deserve justice," she said in an interview with the *Greenwich Citizen*.

Six years before George went missing, twelve-year-old Jaime Decker was brutally raped on a Carnival cruise ship, Marilyn said. The cruise was a family vacation, part of a cross-country adventure for the Deckers.

Five days into the cruise, Jaime was swimming in the pool with a group of other children when a uniformed crewmember asked her if she wanted to see "where the dolphins play." He took Jaime to a restricted area, raped her, and left her lying in a pool of blood, according to Marilyn. He threatened to kill her and her family if she reported the crime, saying he knew her name, where she was from, and what cabin she was staying in.

The terrified child kept the secret until a youth counselor on the ship noticed that she seemed upset. Jaime said a crewmember had "hugged her and frightened her."

The counselor informed Marilyn, who attempted to speak to crewmembers. But they "made it clear that they didn't believe Jaime." They brought the twelve-year-old face to face with a lineup of crewmen so she could identify the man she said had "hugged her and frightened her." "But they told her if she chose the wrong man, she would ruin his life forever," Marilyn said.

The terrified child did not pick out a suspect, and Marilyn said she was "never examined by a ship's doctor, and the crime was never investigated."

Back home, the once well-adjusted child began showing symptoms of post-traumatic stress disorder—claustrophobia, bulimia, flashbacks, nightmares, and anger. But she kept the attack a secret from her family because of her fear that the crewman would kill them.

"We didn't understand her behavior," said Marilyn. "My husband and I have been married for thirty years. We are a stable family. The idea of trauma never entered our minds." Three years later, Jaime confessed the secret to a friend, who told Jamie's family. "Once we knew the truth, the healing could begin," Marilyn said. Jaime received counseling and support from family and friends, but the ramifications of the trauma persisted. "She has come a long way, but she still has symptoms. She cannot be alone. It is still a very long process."

The Deckers sued Carnival Cruise lines and ran into the familiar corporate strategy. At the settlement conference, "they stated their final offer and told our attorney that if we didn't settle, they would send a team of attorneys to our small California town, secure a yearbook from the high school, and start interviewing each student in the hope of digging up any dirt on Jamie and our family," according to Marilyn. Jaime wasn't well enough psychologically to continue the fight, so the family agreed to settle.

The Deckers refused to accept a confidentiality clause, though, often standard procedure in such settlements. "Very few families can talk about these crimes because they accept the confidentiality agreements. But I was never going to sign it. They are never going to silence me," Marilyn said.

Carnival spokesman Vance Gulliksen maintained that the Decker case was "properly handled and fully investigated." He claimed that "Jaime Decker, a minor, told one of the ship's youth counselors that a crewmember took her to a crew-only area at the bow of the vessel and allegedly massaged her back and embraced her to crack her back. The young counselor immediately reported this allegation to the ship's command."

The toll on Jaime Decker has been considerable, according to Marilyn. The lowest moment came when her mother found her curled in the fetal position, saying she wished the rapist had killed her. "It has been a rough road, but she has come a long way," her mother said.

After joining ICV, the Deckers appeared with the Smiths and Ken Carver on the *Montel Williams Show*. At the end of the show, Williams urged the American public not to go on cruises until safety reforms were instituted.

———

The story struck a painful chord with Janet Kelly, despondent after the sudden death of her eighteen-year old daughter, followed by her husband's heart attack and open heart surgery. Kelly decided to go on a "healing" four-day Carnival cruise with some neighbors. "I had hoped to relax, regroup, and return home to my two sons and loving husband of twenty-nine years. This certainly was a long-overdue vacation, but I could never have anticipated what happened," she said, in a report posted on the ICV website.

On the last night of the cruise, Janet stopped at a poolside bar after a show for a drink before dinner. The bartender, who had been "friendly but not overly flirtatious," she said, gave her a drink that had been laced with a drug. Kelly's knees went rubbery, and her mind went blank. She, too, was taken to a crew-only area, where the bartender allegedly raped her before she passed out, according to Kelly's statements in a *Time* magazine article and on the ICV website.

When she got off the ship, Kelly said she reported the crime to local authorities, who told her that only the FBI had jurisdiction over crimes at sea. "But it took the FBI months to investigate and interview the assailant who had raped me," Kelly wrote on the ICV website. "They did not prosecute him because they claimed to not have enough evidence. Yet they had my clothing, the rape kit completed at my local hospital, the individual's identity, and my testimony," she said.

Meanwhile, back home in Phoenix, Kelly was not only emotionally devastated by the rape but also terrified that she had been exposed to HIV. She hired James Walker and filed a civil suit against the cruise line and the bartender who raped her. Eventually Carnival fired him and sent him back home to Jamaica. Astoundingly, though, another cruise line hired him. Walker contacted the company and had the alleged rapist fired again.

In the article in *Time*, Michael Crye said that "despite cases like Kelly's," the incidence of reported crimes is generally low, and that cruise ship employees undergo thorough background checks conducted by the U.S. State Department.

Capt. Bill Wright is also quoted in the article, saying, "We're approximately 30 times safer than American communities in general." He added that Royal Caribbean reports every incident, even petty thefts, to authorities.

Kelly soon joined ICV and told Rep. Chris Shays that she wanted to testify with the Smiths and Carver at the second congressional hearing.

As media coverage spread across the globe, a horrific story came to light in Australia about Dianne Brimble, forty-two, who had saved enough money to take the trip of a lifetime on a cruise, bringing her youngest daughter, Tahlia, age twelve, with her around the South Pacific on the P&O *Pacific Sky*, according to information posted on the ICV website. Brimble's sister and niece joined them.

After dinner on the first night of the cruise, all four went back to the cabin. Brimble kissed her daughter goodnight and then went to the nightclub. The following morning, she hadn't returned to the cabin. At breakfast, her sister had Brimble paged, but she was soon called to the ship's medical center, where she learned that Brimble was dead. Her naked body had been found on the floor of a cabin assigned to four men, according to the ICV website post.

As the cruise continued on to Noumea, in New Caledonia, Dianne's daughter, sister, and niece had to endure two harrowing days aboard the ship before they could disembark and fly home to Australia. Family members in Australia were given no details, told only that Brimble had died. When detectives boarded the ship in Noumea, Brimble's family, including her ex-husband, Mark Brimble, became suspicious about the circumstances surrounding her death.

After several weeks, the family finally learned the details. Dianne's body was found on the floor of Cabin D182, which belonged to four men she had met at the ship's disco the previous night. A toxicology screen showed evidence of gamma-hydroxybutyric acid, or GHB, in her system. The so-called date-rape drug had contributed to her death, according to Mark Brimble in an article in the *Sydney Morning Herald*.

After reading about the Smith case, Mark Brimble joined ICV and became the Australian spokesperson. Mark Robin Wilhelm, the man allegedly last seen with Dianne, was charged with manslaughter, but the Australian government dropped the case against him in April 2010. Wilhelm was, however, convicted of giving Dianne the drug GHB on the cruise, but despite the coroner's testimony that there was enough evidence to satisfy a jury that "known persons" had committed indictable offenses, no charges held. The Brimble family accused the cruise line of a cover-up, and Brimble vowed to fight the system until justice was served and reforms were instituted on cruise ships.

"There is no maritime organization that keeps records of reported crimes onboard cruise ships," said Mark Brimble in the ICV website post. "You may have a ship registered in Bermuda, owned by a company in London, with a passenger from New Zealand, who says she has been sexually assaulted by a person from yet another country. It's an absolute abyss when it comes to what laws apply."

After Dianne's death, P&O cruises said it instituted several reforms, including twenty-hour surveillance cameras, staff training in crime scene management, and the abolishment of commissions on alcohol sales for crew. "There is no doubt that the inquest into the tragic death of Mrs. Brimble put every part of this business under the microscope," said P&O spokesperson Sandy Olsen on the ICV website.

———

These stories were all too familiar to Randy Jaques. The veteran ship security officer and retired Las Vegas cop was working for Holland America Cruises when George Smith went missing, and he followed the media coverage intently. He had seen firsthand what he described as the "lax and ineffective security polices," and he was sick of watching the rape and sexual assault victims "walking down the gangway in tears." The stocky U.S. Air Force veteran, who served tours in Afghanistan, decided to step forward as a whistleblower and gave interviews to the *Greenwich Citizen* and *20/20* in April 2006.

"I am not trying to pound on the industry that I love, only to help make cruise ships safe for all persons, passengers, and crew," he said. Shipboard personnel are "so ill prepared to handle something like the George Smith case. They didn't even interview Clete Hyman, the ear-witness. They also, most importantly, failed to maintain the crime scene. What a blunder."

Although Michael Crye told Congress that there is extensive training for cruise ship security guards, Jaques disputes this. "They are merely hired and sent to their ship without any shipboard training. All training is done hands-on by the security officer, only if he desires to do so." There are no stringent requirements for security personnel. "Anyone who says differently is not stating fact, only fiction."

Despite ever-flowing alcohol and the party atmosphere on cruise ships, there is only a handful of security guards onboard. For a typical cruise ship, with approximately 3,300 passengers and crew, a security staff consists of "one security officer, two assistant supervisors, and six security guards. There is no armed law enforcement officer," says Jaques.

This atmosphere can attract a criminal element, Jaques believes. Another major problem, as seen in the Decker, Kelly, and Brimble cases, comes from the crew themselves. "As soon as women guests come onboard, they are targeted by crewmembers. It's a running joke, which women are single, which are available, who looks good." For parents to send their young daughters alone on a cruise is "the biggest mistake you will ever make."

Some members of the crew are from countries where they "do not have the same moral values concerning the treatment of women that we do." When crewmembers commit crimes, they are sometimes simply sent home to their countries of origin. Many of them are "very poorly skilled, with poor English skills, good at the gangway and maybe guest relations, but that is it."

Sexual assaults are stunningly widespread and not disclosed, says Jaques. "I wonder what the FBI would do if they actually knew how many sexual deviants are serving as crew aboard ships. Crimes such as unwanted touching, sexual misconduct, simple battery, and indecent exposure are simply not reported. Multiply that per ship per week across the globe, and do the math."

If a rape is reported, Jaques said the onboard security staff is not properly trained in using tools such as rape kits. "They are often bungled and mishandled. The FBI and Coast Guard fail to step forward to contest underreporting because they are never kept in the loop to begin with."

The protocol for reporting crimes is also of concern to Jaques. When a crime occurs, he said, the first call goes not to the FBI but to the cruise line's corporate office in Miami. "With many crimes, the FBI is the last to know." After the report goes to the corporate office, Jaques said he has no idea what the report's final destination is.

Although cruise line officials testified about low crime rates before Shays's congressional hearings in December 2005 and March 2006, Jaques disputed their statistics. During his own seven-year tenure as a shipboard security officer on just one ship, he handled "more than fifty sexual assault cases involving both passengers and crew, many of which cruise line management never even reported to authorities. Not a week went by without sexual misdemeanor episodes involving unwanted touching or indecent exposure."

During his tenure, he claims, "thousands of Jane Doe agreements were signed by alleged rape victims in which they settled claims with the cruise lines without reporting the crimes. Many of these agreements also contain confidentiality clauses. The victims may also be offered champagne, free cruises, anything to make it go away."

He credits the Smith family for shining light on the issue. "They are the hand that shook the Tower of Babel. My hat is off to them."

After Jaques's story was printed and aired, the cruise industry moved quickly to defuse his damaging allegations. Michael Crye defended the safety and security on cruise ships: "We have very extensive training programs for our security officers. These often include liaisons for training with certain segments of the FBI, the Coast Guard, and the bomb squad in local jurisdictions."

He maintained that the FBI and the Coast Guard have good working relationships with cruise ships. Vicki Woods, a spokesman for the New Haven FBI, declined comment, citing "the ongoing investigation of the George Smith case."

Crye claimed to have met with officials from the Bahamas Maritime Authority to discuss ways to facilitate greater cohesiveness in crime reporting and "rapid law enforcement response" in coordination with the FBI, the Coast Guard, and the Department of Homeland Security. As for cruise ship crime statistics, Crye claimed, "You are safer onboard a cruise ship than in any community in the U.S. Cruise ships are very, very safe."

Gulliksen, the public relations spokesman for Carnival, also questioned Jaques's charges, saying, "Mr. Jaques worked a couple of contracts onboard Carnival Cruise Lines' ships during a fifteen-month period between November 1991 and March 1993. The security department and its function are vastly different today than thirteen years ago when Mr. Jaques was involved."

"They tried to downplay my experience," Jaques countered, "and again my response is, until they have walked in my shoes, they have nothing to state. You need to work seven days a week, twelve to fifteen hours a day, to feel the whole effect of the job, and deal with three thousand passengers and crew per week." Safety and security problems are actually worse now, he said.

After leaving Holland America, Jaques served another tour in Afghanistan, then joined ICV to help "generate global public awareness about cruise safety."

———

Janet Huggard also was watching the intense media coverage of the George Smith case, which raised her suspicions about the industry. Huggard runs an Internet search business, but when she searched online for answers to questions about disappearances and crimes at sea, she found very little information. The lack of information eventually led her to launch her own website, CruiseBruise.com, which keeps a daily listing of every disappearance and rape on a cruise ship.

The more she studied the case, the more Huggard believed that "the cruising public was not really informed about the dangers that existed. Cruising had been romanticized by *The Love Boat*. I believe *The Love Boat* was representational of cruising perhaps in the '60s and '70s, but things have changed as the mix of passengers has changed."

The main difference, according to Huggard, stems from the way the industry has grown. It has "not only brought in a broader mix of passengers but also added many more crewmembers to the mix from a wider range of backgrounds, creating an immense melting pot of cultures, traditions, education, and agendas."

Disturbed by the Smith case and the ongoing evasiveness of the cruise industry, she launched a victims' advocacy site to serve "the many people who have been victimized by a heartless industry, giving them a chance to be heard."

CruiseBruise.com contains an extensive database of crimes and incidents on cruise ships. It launched on December 13, 2005, shortly after the first Shays hearing. As of March 2011, the site had nearly 10 million page views by 2.5 million visitors. The site lists not only deaths, missing passengers, and sexual assaults on cruise ships but also bedbug infestations, drug busts, fires, epidemics, groundings and sinkings, pirate attacks, mutinies, sanitation reports, travel agent fraud, and stock reports.

Every new cruise crime report or update in a case spikes traffic to her site, "which comes from all over the world. It comes from every company in the cruise industry, the travel industry, major hotel chains, law enforcement, the media, and politicians from the bottom all the way to the top."

Huggard gets tips from victims, attorneys, and other passengers; researches databases; translates foreign documents; and frequently get previews of media articles before they hit the public. She has a handful of informants as well. She also, like the Smiths, endures threats and harassment from unknown persons, she says.

"I've had nasty e-mails from people who claim to work for the cruise industry," she said. "A death threat came from a person who claimed to be a family member of a victim." Still, she refuses to back down and continues to provide daily updates on her site.

———

At Shays's next congressional hearing, in March 2006, the drama intensified. The media frenzy descended on Capitol Hill once again, and John Mica, the congressman from Florida who had defended the industry at the previous hearing, grew irate when he saw the cameras setting up and the overflowing press table. He leaned into the crowd and pointed a finger at a reporter. "Must be a slow news day!"

Several more cruise crime victims and their families joined the Smiths and Carver at the Rayburn Building. Among them was Brian Mulvaney, a relative of fifteen-year-old Lynsey O'Brien, who just a few months prior allegedly had been served ten alcoholic drinks aboard Carnival's *Costa Magica* and while vomiting had fallen overboard.

Before the hearings, both the Smiths and Jennifer held press conferences. The Smiths held theirs in the lobby of the Rayburn Building. Bree spoke first and once again blasted the industry. "Reform is needed so Americans won't have to risk their lives when they take a cruise," she said. "The cruise industry puts profits before human life."

Meanwhile, as a prelude to the hearings, Jennifer had released a list of safety tips for children on cruise ships through her publicist. The tips focused mainly on awareness of potential dangers, warning children to be alert and not wander the ship alone.

Underscoring her points, Jennifer's attorney James Walker added that the "most common victims on cruise ships are women and children." The source of the problem, he said, was "poor pre-employment background checks on crewmembers. A crewmember who is found to be a sexual predator can be fired and sent home by one cruise ship and then picked up by another and rehired. This is because cruise ships don't have to share the same database."

Jennifer also held a press conference, surrounded by her family, at the Hyatt Regency Hotel. Looking tan but conservatively dressed in a black pin-striped pants suit, she eased through the questions from the national media.

Then John Hagel, her father, denounced voluntary reporting. "Every town, city, and state in the U.S. keeps crime statistics." Some cruise lines didn't "even report larcenies under $10,000 because that doesn't meet their threshold."

After Hagel finished, Jennifer's lawyer continued to lace into the cruise lines, using a pointer and chalkboard to illustrate his points. He mentioned the issue of alcohol, saying the cruise lines push the sale of liquor and profit from it. "The evaluations of waiters and servers are based on the volume of alcohol sales."

"We're talking vacations here," Walker said, using his pointer to zero in on the self-reported crime statistics on the chalkboard. "You haven't had anyone disappear from Disney World. If this was Disney World, they'd shut it down."

After condemning the FBI's prosecution record, Walker's speech took a strange turn. He said that Dr. Henry Lee, had "significant forensics evidence not found by either the FBI or the Turkish police" but that the FBI was not cooperating with him. New Haven FBI spokeswoman Vicki Woods wouldn't comment, but Walker's statement raised a glaring question. Lee had been director of the Connecticut State Police Forensic Science Laboratory before going into private practice. Why wasn't the FBI working with a former colleague? Or was it, as George III maintained, another volley in the public relations campaign?

After the press conferences, both groups headed for the hearing room in the Rayburn Building and took their seats. Cameras from the major networks jostled for position, and reporters who couldn't find seats at a press table stood in the back. This time, the Smiths and Jennifer made no pretense of sitting together, keeping several rows between them. The same committee of congressmen faced them.

———

Shays started by reading parts of a ten-point safety plan drafted by Bree Smith, Ken Carver, and other ICV members. The plan called for mandatory reporting of crimes, tighter security checks and screening of crew, and the onboard presence of an independent safety and security force composed of U.S. sea marshals. Shays then read statements by Jennifer and the Smiths endorsing the proposal. He also supported it, explaining how it would help clarify murky waters.

"Good luck to passengers wishing to understand their rights at sea," he said. "Even attorneys find it difficult to navigate the complex jurisdictional boundaries, statutory definitions, treaty provisions, maritime traditions, and fine-print liability disclaimers."

Janet Kelly told the harrowing story of her rape. After Carver testified again, Brian Mulvaney told the story of Lynsey O'Brien, who had fallen overboard while vomiting. "I can't imagine a worse crime than plying a fifteen-year-old girl with so much liquor she literally died as a direct result." Their cruise of a lifetime "turned out to be the worst nightmare imaginable. You don't expect to go on a cruise with four children and come back with only three."

It took fifteen minutes before the ship even began to slow down after Lynsey was known to be missing. "By that time, it had traveled quite a distance from the original location where Lynsey had fallen. There was no effort, whatsoever, on behalf of the ship to lower any lifeboats."

Congressmen Kucinich and Sanders expressed their outrage and pledged to fight for safety reforms. But John Mica had a different view. Unfazed by the testimony, Mica dismissed the notion that more security was needed on cruise ships and once again pointed out that cruise vacations were highly affordable for the middle class. He also discussed the several enjoyable cruises he had taken over the years.

Janet Kelly challenged him, insisting that cruise ships were not safe and that her own experience illustrated this, but Mica continued defending them. George III had been listening to Mica with mounting fury and finally stormed out of the room.

Undeterred, Mica continued his defense of the industry until Mulvaney lost his temper. In an extraordinary scene, he jumped to his feet and told Mica to stop talking immediately. Like a chastened schoolboy, the congressman complied. A tense silence fell over the chamber.

Mica deferred to Crye, who said the ICV ten-point plan was unnecessary and redundant. "All allegations of crimes involving U.S. citizens are reported to the FBI, and alleged crimes against Americans can be investigated and prosecuted under U.S. statutes even if they arise on cruise ships outside U.S. waters."

He didn't explain why there had never been a single successful prosecution of a cruise crime. International law issues onboard cruise ships would complicate matters, according to Crye. "How would U.S. sea marshals know which law to apply?" he asked.

Captain Wright, appearing as cool and dispassionate as ever, claimed that Royal Caribbean already conducted background checks on crew. He said the Smiths' and Jennifer's "media campaign" was fraught with "false and misleading allegations that change by the day." Then he escalated the rhetoric, saying the media campaign had "hampered the FBI investigation." He did not elaborate.

———

After the hearings, Bree expressed her optimism on the *Nancy Grace* television show about the momentum gained by the hearings and the cruise safety bill that would arise from them. "I think that the American public is now aware that the dirty little secrets of Royal Caribbean have finally surfaced, as well as the other cruise lines. The American public will no longer tolerate it, and neither will Congress."

# 15

# SHAKEN LIVES

After the hearings, Jennifer's settlement meetings with Fain and Goldstein, including the strange session in the airport hangar, continued. Neither Walker nor the Smiths knew about these meetings, even though Jennifer was the administrator of George IV's estate. According to Bree, she had told the Smiths that they would file their claims jointly in the wrongful death suit she was pursuing. The purpose of the suit was to force Royal Caribbean to provide more information in the civil discovery process, during which the four men of interest could be deposed.

Jennifer was also starting a new life. Her publicist, Mike Paul, said she was unable to work as a teacher because of the publicity of the case, so she had moved to Boston. She worked as an office manager on Newbury Street and lived in an apartment "filled with George's things," according to Bree.

Then she decided to pursue her "real passion," according to a later statement, and moved to New York City. She took classes in fund-raising and philanthropy at New York University, earning a certificate in the field in 2007. She let her trademark mane of blond hair go brown and started pinning it loosely in the back with a simple barrette. She got a job as major gifts officer in development and donor relations at the Michael J. Fox Foundation for Parkinson's Research. Her biography on the foundation's website indicates that she also serves as board member of the Edwin Gould Academy in Harlem, a nonprofit organization helping homeless youth.

She also found a new boyfriend, Jeff Agne, a financial analyst who grew up in Rocky Hill, a town neighboring Cromwell in Connecticut. Agne was a student at New York University's Stern School of Business. Like Jennifer, he had been a soccer star in high school, leading his team to the state semifinals. He had graduated from the University of Vermont in 2001 and spent time working for AIG and then Factset Management in Stamford.

---

The George Smith case continued to captivate and engage the public. Lifetime TV filmed a made-for-TV movie based on the case, *Deadly Honeymoon,* which aired in April 2010.

The story begins as a party boy from a wealthy family meets a determined girl from the other side of the tracks who gets him to propose to her. On their Hawaiian honeymoon cruise, they spend too much time drinking and gambling with four suspicious young guys, and "Trevor" mysteriously disappears one night. "Lindsey" is found in a hallway, disoriented and unable to remember how she got there. Trevor is missing, and a check of their stateroom shows a broken bottle, some blood around the room, and finally a bloody handprint on the railing outside their stateroom.

The story then takes a surprising twist. In a flashback scene, Lindsey shoves Trevor overboard in a fit of jealous rage and then attempts to make a shady deal to cover up the crime with the captain of the ship. There is also a scene showing Lindsey about to have sex with another man on the night Trevor went missing.

The thinly disguised parallels to the George Smith case fooled no one. Huffington Post blogger Jackie Cooper wrote, "What will draw people to this movie is its close resemblance to the actual case that involved the disappearance of George Smith. . . . The makers of *Deadly Honeymoon* took these facts and used them as a frame for the movie that is now being offered. Whether or not it is actually close to the truth will never be known."

James Walker wasn't happy with the movie. "I had never heard of the Lifetime Movie Network before. Now I know why. The movie is very dramatic. But like most Hollywood productions it is ridiculous, having little to do with the actual facts of the case." Walker said there was partying during George and Jennifer's cruise, but asked, "What cruise ship doesn't have partying and drinking? Was there infidelity? No."

The television series *Haunting Evidence* put two psychics onto *Brilliance of the Seas*, and each offered different versions of what happened. Both agreed that George and Jennifer were drinking heavily and claimed that Jennifer tried to get George jealous by flirting with some of the men they were partying with.

One psychic said the men then walked George to his room and upset him by talking about Jennifer. George fell, hit his head, and was bleeding heavily. He was then thrown off the balcony, which could account for the bloody hand print found on the railing. The psychic said that when she recounted this scenario, the cabin door was opening and shutting under apparently its own accord, underscoring the veracity of her conclusion.

The other psychic simply believed the *Vanity Fair* theory that George was drunk and sitting on the balcony rail before losing his balance and falling overboard.

The case made the E! channel's list of the "20 Most Shocking Unsolved Crimes."

As the story extended across the globe, the international media began covering it more intensively. The *Haaretz Daily*, Israel's largest newspaper, sent reporter Shahar Smooha to Greenwich to interview the Smith family. Smooha said the interest stemmed from both "a human interest and a business angle." Sami Ofer, the eighty-three-year old Israeli patriarch of Royal Caribbean, keeps a home in Tel Aviv and was dealing with the fallout of the storm battering the industry.

After the interview with Smooha, the Smiths appeared on British television on ITV1's *Holidays Undercover,* along with Carver, now ICV president, and Paul O'Brien, father of Irish teen Lynsey. Carver was also interviewed for Channel 9, a national network in Australia, where the story of Dianne Brimble continued to make headlines.

———

Summer warmed the beaches of Greenwich—but not the Smiths. George's absence had created a yawning chasm in their lives. Maureen couldn't tend her garden as she used to. The constant media attention had drawn so many curiosity-seekers that the Smiths had placed a No Trespassing sign on the lawn, once a social hub for family and friends. Bree continued to use her legal skills to fight for her brother's cause and for ICV. George III worked at the family store in Cos Cob, battling his grief as best he could. To the cruise industry's consternation, all of them continued to appear on the talk shows.

Shortly before the first anniversary of George's disappearance, the Smiths held a memorial service at Sacred Heart Catholic Church in the Byram section of Greenwich, where the family had worshipped for generations. Maureen's family flew in from England, and Ken Carver came from Arizona.

Before the service, Carver told a reporter about harassment he was enduring and concerns for his safety. After the hearings, he had experienced disturbing episodes, such as believing he was being followed. Even reporters covering the story were not immune; some had their tires slashed and windshield wipers broken by unknown persons.

The historic brick church with high stained-glass windows was packed to overflowing. Drew Lufkin, George's former fraternity brother at Tau Kappa Epsilon, tried to eulogize his late friend, but the former hockey player struggled to complete nearly every sentence, repeatedly breaking down into sobs. He conveyed George's boisterous sense of humor and his loyalty as a friend. "I miss you, big guy," he said.

At a reception afterward at the Greenwich Country Club, members of Maureen Smith's family gave eulogies about the handsome, high-spirited boy they had called "Georgie."

Afterward, as Maureen, George, and Bree wept, Ken Carver rose gallantly to his feet and raised a glass of champagne.

"To the Smiths," he said. "We are going to win this fight."

---

The midsummer heat shimmered on the asphalt as the Smiths—exhausted from the memorial service, bracing themselves for the exact anniversary of George's disappearance—prepared to file a lawsuit with Brett Rivkind in Miami against Royal Caribbean, charging them with deliberately and intentionally portraying George's death as an accident, hampering an appropriate investigation, inflicting emotional distress, and invading their privacy. They were also awaiting news about the wrongful death lawsuit Jennifer had promised to file.

The Smiths' fax machine came to life with a beep and a ring and a whir of paper. What came out of it stunned them all.

The fax was from James Walker. Bree couldn't believe what she was reading. Jennifer had reached a settlement with Royal Caribbean for $1.1 million. The statement began: "Jennifer Hagel Smith is pleased to announce that she has reached a comprehensive settlement with Royal Caribbean."

*I thank the friends I have stood tall with down in Washington, D.C., as well as the cruise line president and leaders who heard our voices and began this civilized, informative, and productive dialogue. My discussions with Royal Caribbean have been very open, as well as extremely productive and informative. This journey has always been a matter of principle for me, and I know that George would be proud of what has been accomplished thus far, in good faith, as we continue to seek answers. I appreciate Royal Caribbean's cooperation, sincerity and efforts moving forward, which I believe will play a major role in helping all of us find closure. The memory of George will always live on in my heart, that of our families, and everyone who knew him.*

Gone was the acrimony of Jennifer's earlier statements and testimony at the first Shays hearing, where she bemoaned being kicked off the ship in and left to fend for herself in Turkey. In turn, Adam Goldstein praised Jennifer. "She has handled herself well under the most trying of circumstances and we applaud her constructive approach to resolving this matter—so much so that our company will also match a contribution by Ms. Hagel to a charity of her choosing."

Walker, who had vehemently berated the cruise industry in Washington, also defended the settlement, saying Royal Caribbean was providing new information about the night George went missing, including "logs, reports, witness statements . . . and we can look at the surveillance videos, card key reports, and so forth. I have never obtained such a concession from a cruise line before, and I think that this information will provide Jennifer with a lot of answers and should confirm that George was a victim of whom we believe." He did not say who this might be.

News of the settlement spread across the media, and the Smiths' phone started ringing. But they were still reeling from the shock. The announcement came like a bodily blow, especially so close to the anniversary of George's death.

Then shock gave way to anger. The embattled family fought back harder than ever. This time, they ripped off the gloves and exposed all their suspicions about Jennifer—her behavior on the night George went missing and what they perceived to be her lack of forthrightness.

"Jennifer deceived and betrayed us," Bree said later that day to the *Greenwich Citizen*. Not only had Jennifer entered into secret negotiations with Royal Caribbean behind their backs and without their knowledge, but the settlement also threw a roadblock in the pursuit of justice because "it restricted the flow of critical information from the cruise line . . . [that] the civil discovery process would have provided." The settlement also indicated that the Smiths would not be allowed access to all the information unless they dropped their civil lawsuit.

Then Bree turned up the heat. "We feel comfortable in saying that, in our opinion, she is hiding something. Given the extent of her suspicious behavior over the past year, it is not clear to us whether Jennifer is hiding behavior that is just embarrassing or of some greater importance to the investigation. We have reported all such behavior to the FBI as it has occurred."

That night, Bree appeared on the *Nancy Grace* show, which dramatically announced the breaking news in the case, characterizing the settlement as a second cover-up. She explained that the Smiths were depending on Jennifer's lawsuit to open the channels of information, since in their own lawsuit they wouldn't be able to interview and depose the same witnesses.

"Jennifer wants to move on with her life with a large payout," Bree said, "whereas my family wants information as to what happened to George. I don't know what Jennifer is hiding and what Royal Caribbean is hiding that they feel a need to settle this so quickly, but I know that my family are not going away. We will not be settling."

Nancy Grace listened intently as Bree fired off a series of questions to Royal Caribbean: "If your company did nothing wrong, why are you paying Jennifer Hagel anything? My second comment is according to the fax that we just received; it says the information will be provided upon completion of the settlement. Why do we have to settle with your company in order to get information as to what happened to my brother on that ship? You should be forthcoming with that information so my family can find out who murdered George and get justice for him."

Jeffrey Maltzman, whose website client list teems with cruise line companies, appeared on the show with Bree. He had represented Royal Caribbean in such cases as Merrian Carver's. However, on the show he said, "I don't work for Royal Caribbean. I don't know why you're angry at me or, frankly, the cruise line."

Diverting from the topic of the settlement for a moment, he questioned whether a murder had occurred all. "It's the FBI's job to figure out if a crime has happened here. It's not a cruise line's job to be CSI and try to figure those types of things out. And, frankly, most people who hear the facts and story that's come out over the last year don't assume that a murder or a crime did occur."

His statement sparked a dramatic confrontation.

Grace, irate at his comment, jumped in. "Why? Why, Jeffrey? I'll step in. Because I find it very unusual that there's blood inside the stateroom. He fell or was pushed off the balcony, clearly, and the door was closed."

"I think the vast majority of Americans and people worldwide think that a murder was committed on that night," Bree countered. "And Mr. Maltzman can talk and lie through his teeth about the fact there were not any suspicious circumstances, but we know differently. The FBI has a very open and active investigation still. And millions of dollars are currently being spent on this, and it's all because Royal Caribbean did not seal off that crime scene like they said they would. They contaminated it, so when the FBI finally got onboard, they had a very difficult job getting the evidence they need to prosecute this crime."

She continued, backing Maltzman into a corner. "There was more blood in the cabin than Mr. Maltzman would like to admit. We have crime scene photos. Additionally, there was a substantial amount of blood on the overhang. There were also sounds of fighting coming from that cabin. We know that three of the four individuals that brought my brother back to his cabin have taken the Fifth Amendment. I mean, read the writing on the wall, Mr. Maltzman. It doesn't take a genius."

"Well, frankly, I don't understand what relevance blood on the overhang has," he replied. "If somebody falls off a balcony and strikes the overhang, they're going to bleed."

"But what about the argument that ensued just before he went missing, a giant thud, raised voices, and now he's dead?" Grace intervened again.

Maltzman prevaricated. "Well, I've heard reports of an argument. I've heard the passenger in the cabin right next door on the media saying that what he heard sounded like loud partying. I've heard sounds that sounded like thuds and furniture being moved. But it's unclear whether that was being done by George alone in the room or George with other people in the room. And I certainly wasn't there."

Grace asked Greg McCrary, a Royal Caribbean cruise line consultant and former FBI agent: "Isn't it true that the captain of the ship deemed this to be an accident?"

"I believe that was his opinion," McCrary said. "And, certainly, really, his opinion doesn't matter. What he thinks doesn't matter."

"The ship's captain doesn't matter?" Grace asked, incredulous. "Why?"

"What matters—because what counts are the facts and what the criminal investigation shows. What you think and what I think and Bree thinks, none of that matters. What matters are the facts."

"But he's in charge of the ship and the investigation," Grace pointed out.

"Well, that doesn't give him clairvoyant powers to know what happened. He may have an opinion."

Grace shook her head in disbelief. "That's like saying what the chief of police says doesn't matter. That's a disconnect. That's not making any sense."

---

The next night, Bree appeared on *The Abrams Report* with Susan Filan, the former Connecticut prosecutor. Filan questioned the "love fest" between Jennifer and Royal Caribbean. Bree responded by invoking her brother's memory. "I wonder what George would think of Jennifer taking money without getting answers and becoming the poster child for the cruise line after how they have treated him, his crime scene, and his family."

For them, it wasn't about money. "We would have been happy with a one-cent jury verdict if Royal Caribbean was found liable for their wrongdoing and we were able to find out the tragic circumstances surrounding his death."

———

As headlines spread, Walker jumped to Jennifer's defense, saying Jennifer had "passed a polygraph by the FBI" and that the FBI had "released a statement long ago that Jennifer fully cooperated."

Jennifer herself struck back in a press release, calling the Smiths' statements "misplaced anger and resentment." Her father also stepped forward in her defense. He charged that the Smiths' appeal of the settlement was financially motivated in part because the Smiths claimed the agreement undervalued George's estate.

"I'm not the guy going around saying they want more money," Hagel said in an interview with the *Greenwich Post.* "They are saying this." Hagel also questioned the foul play theory, saying in a press release, "To date, we have not been provided with any evidence that points to foul play."

The battle brewed in the press, and the Smiths marked the anniversary of George's disappearance on July 4 by planting a ruby-red horse chestnut tree in his memory at Strickland Brook Park in Greenwich. George had ridden his bicycle there on his way to the liquor store, and had been able to see the park from the window of the store.

The event was open to the town of Greenwich. Despite the July heat and the long-standing tradition of many Greenwich residents to vacation at that time of year, the somber ceremony drew a large crowd, including Congressman Shays and the ubiquitous media.

Maureen read a statement, both sorrowful and determined. Composing himself, George III also read a statement, thanking Shays for intervening when George disappeared and helping obtain critical information. "Without Chris Shays, so much would have been swept under the carpet," George said.

Then it was Shays's turn. The incumbent congressman was fighting a battle for reelection against charismatic Democrat Diane Farrell. To make matters worse, both the cruise industry and members of his own party were reportedly pressuring Shays to stop the hearings and the fight for the bill. Shays refused.

He spoke passionately about the cause. "I am outraged about how the Smiths were dealt with by the cruise industry as family. Their work with ICV is an attempt to make sure that other families will not be dealt with in the same way . . . and the work of the Smith family has awakened a whole nation."

The Smiths tossed shovelfuls of dirt onto the tree.

After the ceremony, when Shays was asked what it would take to get his stalled bill passed in Congress, he shook his head and said, "It's probably going to take another tragedy." Unfortunately he was right.

———

Jennifer's life took a sharp new path after the settlement. Not only did she and her family stop blasting Royal Caribbean but she also worked in conjunction with them, giving the keynote speech at the Family Assistance Foundation's annual conference in Atlanta in 2008. Royal Caribbean, Carnival, and other cruise lines sponsored the event.

The FAF describes itself as

> *an independent nonprofit corporation founded in 2000 for the purpose of empowering people following tragedy. Our mission is to support and improve business and industry responses to emergencies and disasters. The Foundation takes a unique, research-based approach to helping organizations successfully meet survivors' (customers, affected families, employees, any member of the public impacted) needs by coordinating and mobilizing resources during the acute phase of a crisis and beyond.*

Jennifer's keynote address focused on her own story and the power of FAF. She was introduced with the following description:

*In July of 2005, Jennifer Hagel and George Smith were married in a storybook wedding near the water in . . . Rhode Island. After visiting dream vacation spots such as the South of France and Rome, while approaching the coast of Turkey, Jennifer awoke to learn that George had gone missing sometime while she slept. Jennifer will share her story and talk about the power that an organization that empowers its employees to help can have in assisting a family survivor find renewed hope for life. We hope that you will join us this year and learn from Jennifer and others about the impact that you and your team members can have on the lives of everyone who goes through tragedy.*

To Ken Carver, the FAF was mere window dressing. "Frankly, the cruise lines have used it to show that they are doing something, and they are not," he said.

## 16

# MOUNTING PRESSURES

Cruise crime victims continued stepping forward. In nearly every case, there were disturbing parallels with the George Smith case about cruise line protocol when responding to missing passengers or shipboard crimes and disasters.

Jamie Barnett's daughter, Ashley, a twenty-four-year-old aspiring actress, had vanished from a Carnival cruise in October 2005. Barnett claimed in an interview with the *Greenwich Citizen* that the cruise line failed to provide meaningful assistance and had refused to interrupt the trip or secure the ship, even when Ashley was reported missing. Barnett had hired defense attorney Gloria Allred, who represented Nicole Brown Simpson's family during the O. J. Simpson murder trial, to sue the cruise line to find answers.

After watching the coverage of the George Smith case and the congressional hearings, Barnett, head of the grip department at CBS Studios in Studio City, California, joined ICV and appeared with the Smiths on *48 Hours*.

Ashley Barnett had been the music coordinator for composer John Debney, who had scored the films *Bruce Almighty* and *The Princess Diaries*. Debney said he never imagined he would lead an orchestra at Ashley's funeral. Jamie Barnett recounted how Ashley had taken a Mexican cruise vacation on the *Paradise* from Long Beach with her boyfriend, Geoff Ginsburg, to celebrate her twenty-fifth birthday. She was dead the next day.

According to Ginsburg, he and Ashley went to the casino and a concert and then returned to their cabin. At 2:30 a.m. they allegedly had a "disagreement." Ginsburg returned to the casino, while Ashley retired for the evening.

Ginsburg returned to the cabin at 4:00 a.m. and joined Ashley, who seemed to be sleeping. He woke early the next afternoon and went upstairs to join some friends, leaving the still sleeping Ashley to get some rest. When he came back to the cabin at 2:00 p.m., he tried unsuccessfully to wake her. He ran into the hallway, screaming that his girlfriend wasn't breathing. Another passenger heard his cries and told him to call 911.

A nurse arrived and began CPR on Ashley. An emergency public address broadcast summoned the ship's doctor. The doctor arrived, but efforts to resuscitate Ashley were unsuccessful. According to the ship's records, she was pronounced dead at 2:45 p.m.

At around 6:00 p.m. Barnett learned of her daughter's death from the ship's nurse, who had no answers to the distraught mother's questions. "I demanded to speak with her boyfriend, but I was told that he was currently in questioning. Later I was informed that he had been cleared from the questioning but declined to speak with me."

Because the boat was docked in Ensenada, Mexican authorities boarded the ship to determine if a homicide had been committed. The FBI was also notified. Later that night, with Ginsburg and the other passengers still aboard, the *Paradise* set sail.

"Though the ship was scheduled to return to Long Beach within thirty-six hours, Ashley was left behind, alone in a Mexican morgue," Barnett said.

The following day, Ginsburg called Jamie, saying he didn't know what happened, but some of his medications were missing—methadone and Vicodin. When the ship returned to Long Beach, the FBI began its own investigation and asked Barnett to remain at the harbor. "I stood in the rain for four hours. Finally the agents interviewed me; however, they revealed very little."

Five days after her death, Ashley's body returned to the United States. Getting her home had proved "both tedious and torturous." Confused by the lack of answers and information, Barnett hired a private pathologist to conduct a forensic autopsy. According to Barnett, his report showed that Ashley's organs were "healthy and her body was in pristine condition, with some evidence of alcohol consumption. There were no signs of trauma. Weeks later we learned the cause of death. Ashley died of the toxic effects of methadone."

Barnett was stunned. "Ashley was adamantly antidrug, and she would never have knowingly taken methadone. To prove this, we requested a test of Ashley's hair follicles. The results were clear. No drugs, including methadone, were found in her beautiful, long hair. The test was unequivocally 'negative' for habitual drug use."

So how did the drug end up in Ashley's body? Ginsburg claimed that he never gave her the drug, and its presence in her system remains a mystery. "Despite four trips to meet with the authorities in Ensenada, Mexico, we have no answers. To date, the FBI investigation remains open, but to our knowledge no continuing action is under way."

Carnival released a statement to the *Los Angeles Times*, saying the crisis was handled appropriately. "Tragically, Ashley Barnett died of a drug overdose and was deceased well before medical assistance was summoned," the statement said. "The cruise line's medical professionals responded rapidly, appropriately, and professionally, and the suit is completely without merit."

Ashley Barnett's story generated widespread media coverage. *CBS News* reported the story by saying, "The cruise ship industry faces another blow with the death of Ashley Barnett, who died during a Carnival cruise last October. Her family said the cruise line is stonewalling."

————

The family of Amy Lynn Bradley also joined ICV. Amy Lynn, twenty-four, vanished from a Caribbean cruise she was on with her parents and her brother on Royal Caribbean's

*Rhapsody of the Seas* in 1998. The story contained similar elements to nearly all the stories of persons missing from cruise ships. Amy Lynn left her cabin during the early morning and never returned. According to a statement from her family on the ICV website, certain crewmembers had been "overly attentive" toward Amy during the cruise.

After dinner one night, one of the waiters said he wanted to take Amy to Carlos and Charlie's Club while docked in Aruba, but she allegedly declined. Later Amy mentioned that the waiter "gave her the creeps." The last person seen with her the morning she vanished was a cruise ship band member, known as "Yellow," from a group called Blue Orchid.

When her family realized she was missing, they begged personnel at the purser's desk to back the ship from the dock and secure all gangways. They refused. As in so many other cases, the ship continued on its scheduled itinerary.

The family said they pleaded with the supervisor of the purser's desk to make an announcement that Amy was missing and post her picture. "Only a customary announcement was made: 'Amy Bradley, please contact the purser's desk.'" Soon after, "the captain of the cruise ship told us that he would not make an announcement that she was missing or post a photo for others passengers to view, as this would disturb the other guests."

The Bradleys went to view photos taken of passengers and posted on Deck 4. All the ones of Amy had been removed. The crewman in charge of the photo gallery said he remembered placing Amy's with the others but didn't know what happened to them. The family asked if he could have them reprinted, and he agreed, saying they would be available the next day. They never received them. The family still has the order ticket.

According to the family's statement, the captain told the Bradleys that every nook and cranny of the ship had been searched, but the FBI had different information. The day after Amy went missing, while the Bradleys were in a hotel in Curacao, the FBI told them that the shipboard search had only included the common areas and restrooms.

The shocked and grief-stricken family flew from Curacao and met the ship in St. Maarten. "We demanded a meeting with the captain and chief of security."

As in the Smith case, "the cruise line's 'risk management agent,' or lawyer, had arrived," they said. The Bradleys called the FBI again, and the cruise line attorney was present during their interviews with the agents. He was also present during all other interviews—yet the Bradleys were prohibited from attending the interviews, they said.

On *America's Most Wanted,* the FBI said they found no reason for Amy to leave her family or cause harm to herself.

"After our precious daughter, Amy, our heart, disappeared on March 24, 1998, we received absolutely no help, none, from anyone in that cruise company from that moment on," said Iva Bradley, in a comment to the *Greenwich Citizen* in December 2006.

According to a report on CNN's *Nancy Grace: Cold Cases* in January 2011, a jawbone was found on a beach in Aruba, leading to speculation that it could be linked to Amy's disappearance. In the report, Ron and Iva said, "We believe our daughter is alive, but being held captive by someone," and mentioned a witness sighting of Amy in a department store restroom in Barbados in 2005, which they considered credible.

The Nancy Grace show reported that Royal Caribbean did not respond to their request for a comment, and authorities in Curacao and Aruba said the investigations remain open.

———

The family of Annette Mizener also joined ICV and reported similarly suspicious circumstances with crewmembers and a botched search effort. Annette disappeared from the Carnival cruise ship *Pride* on a Mexican Riviera cruise in December 2004. Although Annette had been reported missing, the ship failed to conduct an immediate search for her. "The captain did not drop rescue boats or turn the ship around for approximately two and a half to three hours, and only upon being ordered to do so by the Coast Guard," her husband, John Mizener, said in a statement posted on the ICV website.

The family also discovered that Annette's purse was removed from the scene and then later returned to its original location, wiped clean of fingerprints. Also according to Mizener, "No pictures were taken of the crime scene, despite the presence of Carnival's . . . security personnel."

———

Nancy Nelson also suffered tragedy on a cruise ship and stepped forward after seeing coverage of the George Smith case. In November 2001 she and her husband, Bob, took a Royal Caribbean cruise to the Bahamas on the *Sovereign of the Seas*.

While on the cruise, Bob purchased a shore excursion through the cruise line to go scuba diving. He left the ship that morning for his scuba adventure on a choppy, whitecapped sea. It was the last time Nancy saw him.

Because of rough seas, all the other dive companies had canceled their dives, and "no one should have been out diving," she said in an interview with the *Greenwich Citizen*. The dive master, Bob's "diving buddy," left him to help another diver with his equipment, and Bob sank to his death at the bottom of the ocean.

Once again, there was no urgency to conduct a search, according to their son Mark Nelson, who flew to the Bahamas immediately after hearing of his father's disappearance. "The Bahamian government had not informed the U.S. Coast Guard, but the Coast Guard was requesting permission to search," he said in a statement on the ICV website. They did not obtain that permission until the following day. This may have been due to the dive company's delay of several hours in reporting my father as missing. Apparently they waited until they did their own unsuccessful search before reporting his disappearance. By then, it was too dark to continue searching."

Unsatisfied, the Coast Guard wanted to conduct another search, but the Bahamian government denied the request, Mark claims. "So by Saturday night nobody was looking for my father! My mother was so hysterical that she needed to be medicated."

In the meantime, "my sister-in-law was calling the hospitals and morgues, all of which were completely full due to a recent hurricane. As a result, she was forced to search through John Does and others on her own," Mark said.

When the family returned home, Mark contacted Royal Caribbean to request a copy of the report on his father's accident but was told "there was no report and nothing on file." Nancy fought Royal Caribbean in court, but her lawsuits failed because her husband had signed a waiver and Royal Caribbean didn't own the scuba diving company.

In a television interview in Jacksonville, Florida, Nancy said, "Neither the cruise line nor the excursion dive group in the Bahamas ever took responsibility for my husband's disappearance."

A representative for Royal Caribbean contacted the news station to say that Robert Nelson's disappearance was "a tragic accident and that [their] sympathy goes out to the family."

———

Along with a fresh light on past cases, new tragedies drew a volume of media attention the cruise industry had never experienced before.

In late March 2006, shortly after the hearings, Richard Liffridge, his wife, Victoria, and some friends took a Caribbean cruise on Carnival's *Star Princess* out of Port Everglades, Florida, to celebrate Richard's birthday.

At 3:10 a.m. one morning, a fast-moving fire broke out and swept through passenger Decks 9 through 12. More than one hundred cabins were destroyed, including Richard's and his friends'. According to Richard's daughter, Lynette Hudson, her stepmother, Victoria, woke Richard, and they tried to escape, but "thick black toxic smoke began to fill the corridors and seep under the door of their cabin. Once they opened their cabin door, they were unable to see because of the wall of smoke. They got down on their hands and knees and tried to crawl toward an exit."

According to Ms. Hudson, there was no emergency lighting to aid them or any emergency response team to assist them. Victoria held on to the back of Richard's T-shirt as he attempted to lead them through the corridor to safety. But then the ship shifted and threw her to the opposite side of the corridor against the wall. Victoria tried futilely to find her husband but couldn't call out for him because smoke was filling her lungs. Then she heard Richard cry, "Vicky, don't let me die."

They were his last words.

Not long after, Hudson said she noticed an article online that claimed her father had died from a heart attack. The cause of the fire was reported as a smoldering cigarette. The article listed a toll-free number for family members to call for more information, but when Lynette called she was told they didn't have any information. She called back and insisted that someone provide information to her. "I was put on hold so they could verify my information. Finally someone told me that Vicky was in a hospital, being treated for smoke inhalation, and I was able to reach her."

Despite all the bureaucratic runaround, Hudson was listed as her father's emergency contact. "They had my contact information in case of an emergency and did not use it." Meanwhile, her father's body remained in Jamaica.

Carnival reported the cause of Richard's death as a heart attack, but a subsequent autopsy revealed the cause of death as smoke inhalation. The cruise line offered a full refund and a 25 percent discount on a future cruise to passengers on the cruise. They also paid for transportation home and lodging during that transition. But they wouldn't pay to return Richard's remains to his family. "They were focused on taking care of people who were inconvenienced, not on the family of the man who died."

A full week later, the Liffridge family themselves paid for his body to be flown to Atlanta so they could finally start the process of a memorial service.

According to Hudson, the external areas of the ship were not required to have fire extinguishers, sprinklers, or smoke detectors. "We also know that it took one and a half hours to fight the fire due to the construction and partitioning of the balcony areas. We know that highly combustible materials were used on the balconies, and the balcony partitions were manufactured from a polycarbonate material that produced large amounts of dense black smoke."

Princess Cruise Lines, the subsidiary of Carnival that operates the ship, never contacted Hudson or her family. "We still have not received a note, phone call, or sympathy card from Princess Cruise Lines. It is as if this never happened."

Hudson and her family joined ICV and also formed a nonprofit foundation in her father's name. The foundation seeks to enhance fire safety regulations as well as safety in general on cruise ships.

Hudson testified before a third round of congressional hearings. "By the year 2010 twenty million passengers will sail on cruise ships. Visions of these passengers flicking their cigarettes over the rails as unsuspecting passengers are asleep in their cabins, with no fire detectors or sprinklers, instantly comes to mind," she said.

According to a *Wall Street Journal* article on September 13, 2006, a cigarette was determined to be the likeliest cause of the fire. The fire spread to "partitions used for balconies on the ship made of plastic that burn easily and produce thick, black smoke."

After the fire that claimed Richard's life, cruise companies began replacing the dividers. "It fell under our radar screen and the experts throughout the world," said Ted Thompson, ICCL's excecutive vice president, in the *Wall Street Journal*. The *Star Princess* was subsequently fitted with aluminum balcony partitions. "Our goal it to make sure we have the highest level of fire protection onboard our ships," said Julie Benson, a spokesperson for Princess Cruises.

On May 15, 2006, Daniel DiPiero, a twenty-one-year old aspiring pilot on a cruise with friends, went missing from Royal Caribbean's *Mariner of the Seas* in Bahamian waters.

At 2:16 a.m., according to his family's statement posted on the ICV website, shipboard video surveillance cameras showed Daniel falling over the railing into the sea. The DiPieros said that they were first notified that Daniel was missing at approximately 6:00 p.m., more than fifteen hours later. They planned immediately to fly to the nearest port, St. Thomas, still holding out hope that he might be rescued.

As they were about to leave their home the next morning, "We received another phone call. For the first time, we were told a surveillance video had been viewed, and it showed Daniel standing by the rail and falling into the sea." They soon learned from the FBI "that one of the bartenders had stopped serving drinks to Daniel that evening. Daniel and the boys proceeded to another bar onboard the ship, where Daniel was able to obtain additional drinks."

Daniel left his friends around midnight and went out onto the deck of the vessel. He fell asleep on a deck chair, also captured on surveillance cameras. He awoke at 2:15 a.m., walked to the railing, apparently vomiting, then slid over the rail into the sea.

After the cruise line learned Daniel was missing, they allegedly failed to review the surveillance videotapes promptly. As a result, there was a significant delay in notifying the authorities that Daniel was missing. Any rescue efforts that took place happened many hours too late, according to his family's statement.

The saddened, angry family demanded answers, and the cruise line provided some information until the family started asking the kinds of questions raised by ICV at the last round of hearings, "such as the rail heights, security standards, questions about why the video surveillance cameras were not monitored." An attorney instructed the cruise line representatives not to answer any more questions. The cruise line denied the charge made by the DiPiero family.

Daniel DiPiero's disappearance ignited such a media storm that his sister Kate said, "This is not how he would have wanted to be famous."

In an article on Youngstown, Ohio, news website, the DiPiero family announced a personal injury lawsuit against Royal Caribbean. The cruise line declined to comment on "specific allegations" in the suit, but said they "extend their deepest sympathies to the family and friends of Daniel DiPiero."

The Smiths and Carver welcomed the new members into ICV and vowed to continue the fight for a law requiring safety and security reforms on cruise ships. Shays promised to conduct more hearings.

———

Alaska's serene, glacier-sculpted waters draw increasing numbers of cruise ships. Some thirty ships from thirteen lines, including Royal Caribbean and Carnival, sail in the icy seas. More than five hundred cruises a summer bring approximately one million tourists north into the fragile environment. With the rise in cruising have come reports of alleged dumping, raising concern among environmentalists. In 2006 Gershon Cohen of the Campaign to Safeguard America's Waters (CSAW) attempted to leverage the publicity about the cruise industry to fight the polluters. Cohen's battle took twists and turns he never imagined when the cruise industry responded with fierce opposition.

"The cruise lines have been convicted of numerous felonies for purposely dumping hazardous and conventional wastes, yet they remain the least-regulated dischargers into public waters," Cohen said in an interview with the *Greenwich Citizen*. Because cruise ships carry approximately three to five thousand passengers and crew, the ships create "as much waste as a small town," including around "30,000 gallons of sewage, or black water; 255,000 gallons of gray water from kitchens, showers, and laundries; and tons of solid waste." Most ships discharge gray and black water into the ocean, he said.

Norwegian Cruise Line pleaded guilty to falsifying records to cover up illegal dumping in Alaska in 2001. In 2004 Norwegian admitted that a ship accidentally dumped forty thousand gallons of wastewater into the Juan de Fuca Strait in Washington State's Puget Sound.

Cohen and a handful of allies launched the Cruise Ship Ballot Initiative (CSBI) to tax and monitor the cruise industry.

The CSBI required that cruise ships meet all of Alaska's pollution standards like every other industrial and municipal discharger. Onboard ocean rangers would verify compliance.

The CSBI also aimed to establish a tax of $50 per passenger on cruise ships to help maintain docks, waterfronts, and emergency services used by the industry so that local communities wouldn't bear the whole burden of supporting tourism facilities. Cruise lines would have to pay income taxes to Alaska on all Alaska-based revenue, including gambling receipts.

However, before Alaskans went to the polls, the cruise industry struck back. "The cruise industry tried buying the recent election in Alaska by giving a front group $15,000 a day to claim the initiative was a 'punitive' attack on the entire Alaska tourism economy. The words *cruise ship* never appeared in many of the ads, but the public wasn't fooled; the industry's fear campaign ran aground."

According to Cohen, the cruise industry's campaign didn't add up. "Few people believed a $50-a-head tax would decrease cruise traffic or spending in Alaska," Cohen said. "A typical one-week cruise, including cruise ticket, costs $3,500, plus airfare, plus shopping, plus tours, plus alcohol, plus casino gambling."

Alaskan voters passed the CBSI in 2006 by a slender margin, approximately 52 percent to 48 percent. But the cruise industry wasn't finished and didn't cooperate with the ocean rangers or other terms of the initiative.

Ocean Rangers Program Manager Paul Johnson filed a report with the Alaska Department of Environmental

Conservation (DEC) that alleged multiple violations of the new law. Rangers weren't being allowed in certain areas of the ships and were not permitted to interact sufficiently with ship personnel or to view ship logbooks.

Other CSAW members claimed that the cruise industry was bullying Alaska, threatening the state with pulling cruise ships if wastewater standards and other strict environmental rules in the initiative were not relaxed. In 2009 the Alaska legislature amended the law passed by the voters, giving cruise ship operators until the end of 2015 to comply with the initiative. The head tax was reduced by 25 percent, and some pollution regulations were relaxed.

The *Juneau Empire* newspaper reported that cruise industry officials said they were pleased and appreciated the new wastewater discharge rules. The paper also reported that the DEC had removed Cohen from the state's wastewater panel.

"The cruise lines ended up getting almost everything they wanted," said Cohen, who vowed to continue the fight.

———

In a similar case, the *Harmony*, a 940-passenger Japanese-owned ship that sails regularly along the Alaskan coast, discharged 34,600 gallons of sewage and bilge water into California's Monterey Bay National Marine Sanctuary in 2003. Because it took place fourteen miles offshore, the dumping was not illegal, but it violated a voluntary agreement between the cruise line and the California town. According to an article in the *New York Times,* The Crystal *Harmony* had dumped the wastewater near a sea otter refuge despite a "pledge" to Monterey officials. "The Crystal *Harmony* is no longer welcome in Monterey," Carl Anderson, the city's public facilities director said to the *New York Times.* "We mean business and we will do whatever it takes to protect our sanctuary." Michael W. Coleman, a Carnival spokesperson, said the dumping was not reported until February 27 because "there was no requirement to report it." The Monterey City Council voted to ban the *Harmony* and other Crystal Cruises ships from its harbor for fifteen years.

State Senator Joe Simitian was shocked by the fact that Crystal Cruises spoke of how they hadn't broken the law because the dumping took place fourteen miles offshore. "I remember picking up the paper and thinking, *You gotta be kidding me.* Their answer was 'We didn't break any rules.' I remember thinking, *If this isn't against the law, it ought to be.*"

Simitian had better luck with an initiative similar to Alaska's in the California legislature. In 2005 he sponsored a bill banning sewage discharges from cruise ships and commercial ships larger than three hundred gross tons into state waters. The bill passed and was signed into law by Governor Arnold Schwarzenegger, giving California some of the strictest laws in the nation limiting pollution. The new law covers the entire California coastline.

However, the state assembly tabled a 2008 bill sponsored by Simitian to place ocean rangers on cruise ships, and the bill failed to get out of committee. "Buyer beware when you climb on a cruise ship. You're on your own," Simitian said to the *Los Angeles Times,* furious at lobbying by the cruise industry at a pitch and level he had never seen before.

The Obama administration added more safeguards in August 2010, with new federal regulations banning cruise vessels and large commercial ships from discharging sewage within three miles of U.S. coastlines. In a statement, the Environmental Protection Agency (EPA) said the ban "will keep about twenty million gallons of sewage out of coastal waters annually." It applies to ships weighing more than three hundred tons and gives the Coast Guard the authority to cite vessels for violations.

Michael Crye responded that the new ban won't affect cruise vessels because the ships already follow a nondischarge policy as strict as the federal guidelines. Newer ships offer better waste-treatment systems that "can treat effluent to near–drinking water quality." Ships store the sewage in large holding tanks until it is discharged at municipal wastewater treatment facilities or eventually emptied offshore, he said.

———

Negative publicity continued to take a bruising toll on cruise line stock values. Royal Caribbean's fell from a high of $56 in 2004 to a new low of $34 in August 2006. "Every dollar their stock goes down costs the shareholders of Royal Caribbean $210 million dollars," said Carver. "That means that their stock drop has cost shareholders about $4.6 billion dollars. If I were a shareholder, I would say to the management that we need to cooperate with the ICV safety proposals to assure the public that we are concerned with these safety issues."

Instead the cruise industry came north to New York City to hold a press conference at the Millennium Broadway Hotel. Set on West Forty-fourth Street's Club Row—home to the Harvard, Princeton, and New York Yacht Clubs— the hotel mirrored the opulence of the cruise ships. A large gathering of national media was served a gourmet breakfast and lunch.

The press conference began with cruise line officials painting a rosy picture of the "continued growth" of the industry in New York City and Miami and thirty other homeports. Six new ships had joined the fleet, accommodating some "fifty-one million cruisers" in the United States, representing 17 percent of the population, according to the leather-bound book of information provided to the press. Of these cruisers, the average age tipped to forty-nine, changing the image of the typical passengers from newlyweds to "the nearly dead," terms used by Richard Fain and others to describe typical cruise ship passengers.

Cruises were described as the "best vacation value" and the best way to see the world while relaxing in comfort. But there was an elephant in the luxury conference suite: the George Smith case.

After the opening session, Crye tackled the issue with a talk titled "Safety in the Spotlight: Stories of missing passengers, congressional hearings on the safety of cruise ships, a shipboard fire—signs of bigger issues or a bad year for the cruise industry? Find out what the cruise industry is doing to ensure the safety and security of its passengers, crew, and vessels."

As the tension in the room heightened, the stone-faced Crye said, "Last July, George Smith went missing from his honeymoon cruise." He paused for a second as cameras and notebooks snapped into action. Then he repeated his statements from the hearings, saying that despite the tragedy, cruise ships "are very, very safe" and that they work in coordination with the FBI and the Coast Guard when a crime occurs. Therefore, he said, there was no need for the cruise industry to adopt the ICV safety reforms. After his speech, Crye took only a few softball questions, then announced that lunch was being served.

Soon after, the industry—and Crye—underwent reorganization, merging the ICCL into the Cruise Lines International Association (CLIA). Crye became executive vice president, with Terry Dale serving as president and CEO.

Along with the extravagant press conference, the industry was also drafting a sweeping public relations campaign and reputation management program so ambitious that it later came under fire for ethical questions. The newly hired team working on the strategy included Eric Ruff, formerly press secretary to former defense secretary Donald Rumsfeld. Ruff had experienced unwanted publicity of his own after leaving a napkin at a Starbucks in Washington, D.C., on which he had written talking points for Rumsfeld—and a map to Rumsfeld's house.

CLIA hired Washington public relations firm John Adams Associates, known for its experience in crisis communications. John Adams Associates had represented Alyeska Pipeline Service Company, which was under federal investigation after a 2010 spill leaked about 190,000 gallons of oil at a pump station near Delta Junction, Alaska.

The PR firm proposed an extensive reputation management program and outreach plan to counteract the bad publicity caused by the Smith case, ICV, and the congressional hearings. Lanie Fagan, CLIA director of communications, attempted to send the extensive plan to Eric Ruff but inadvertently sent it instead to the *Greenwich Post.*

The strategy, which sounded more like a battle plan in a theater of war, called for mobilizing travel agents, industry suppliers, and possible "new allies, to include Coast Guard and other government agencies in port cities; additional conservation and moderate environmental groups willing to act as advisers and supporters; nontraditional allies such as the Sea Cadets [a youth organization] and the AARP." These allies would then be trained to deliver positive messages about the industry to Congress and the media.

"Events in Washington will be arranged where they will visit their members and receive various perks such as a visit to the White House, a briefing at the State Department, tour and briefing at the Defense Department, and dinners with their senators and top administration officials," the memo said.

The new allies would take on lobbying roles and be asked to blanket target media with op-ed columns, including such publications as *Parade, USA Today, New York Times, Wall Street Journal, Business Week, Time, Newsweek, The Economist,* and the *Christian Science Monitor.*

The controversy didn't stop one of CLIA's members, Royal Caribbean, from launching another public relations counteroffensive. The beleaguered cruise line marched straight into another controversy about their use of "Royal Champions" on cruise websites. According to Consumerist .com, the champions were a group of fifty to seventy-five bloggers organized by Royal Caribbean and rewarded with free cruises and other perks for posting positive reviews at various sites without revealing their affiliations.

Consumerist.com reported that Royal Caribbean worked with Nielsen Buzz Metrics to identify their online supporters. Some fifty cheerleaders were chosen for the quality and quantity of their posts on various topics. Along with free cruises, the Royal Champions were rewarded with invitations to the pre-inaugural sailing parties on *Liberty of the Seas* in New York and Miami in May 2007. It was the first time in company history that ordinary people were invited to such events rather than just VIPs, corporate executives, or top travel agents.

The media, including *USA Today,* got wind of the Champions and interviewed Bill Hayden, Royal Caribbean's associate vice president. Hayden acknowledged that the Royal Champions existed and received perks, including invitations to free two-night preview cruises. But he denied that Royal Caribbean asked them to promote their brand at online sites in return.

By August 2009, however, Royal Caribbean had disbanded the controversial Champion program, replacing it with "social networking outlets."

# 17

# Court Drama

Back in Greenwich, the Smiths narrowed their battle for justice. They were now fighting on two fronts: the civil lawsuit against Royal Caribbean in Miami and seeking to overturn Jennifer's settlement in Greenwich Probate Court. They had stopped appearing on talk shows to prepare for court and avoid tipping their hands.

To finance their mounting legal fees, the Smiths sold the family home in Newport—the last place they saw George alive. George III worked at the store on days that grief didn't lay him low. Bree and Maureen continued devoting their time to George IV's cause—and they were going to need all the strength they could muster.

They faced a tough challenge with the Miami-Dade circuit judge who was going hear their case. Judge Jon Gordon was known to sympathize with the cruise lines. In the late '90s he ruled that a Carnival ship was not responsible for the shipboard doctor's alleged negligence, a ruling later reversed by an appeals court.

A fourteen-year-old girl became ill with abdominal and lower back pain and diarrhea aboard *Ecstasy of the Seas*, according to Charles Lipcon, the attorney who represented the girl and her family. She saw the ship's doctor, Mauro Neri, several times over the course of a few days. Dr. Neri told the family that she had the flu, gave her antibiotics, and assured them that she did not have appendicitis.

The family left the cruise and went home, where the girl was diagnosed with a ruptured appendix. Gordon ruled that Carnival was not responsible for Neri's actions. The Third District Court of Appeals disagreed, however, determining that cruise lines are responsible for the doctors they hire, which extended their liability in medical-malpractice cases.

Judge Gordon was presiding over the Smith case, in which Royal Caribbean's lawyers went further than ever, claiming the cruise line "exceeded its legal requirements when it contacted the FBI and other authorities immediately after learning about Smith's disappearance."

Judge Gordon sided with Royal Caribbean and dismissed the Smiths' case on October 16, 2006, "with prejudice," which meant the suit couldn't be refiled, though it could be appealed.

"It's a setback," Brett Rivkind said, "but not the end."

The Smiths vowed to appeal. They knew it had been a long shot to win in Miami, the cruise industry's backyard, so they were gearing up for the probate battle, which they thought they had a good shot at winning. If they succeeded, they would overturn Jennifer's $1.1 million settlement, which Maureen described as "blood money," and remove her as administrator of George's estate. Then they would file a wrongful death suit on George's behalf against the cruise line, in which they could finally depose witnesses.

———

Maureen Smith woke early on the first day of the probate trial. Outside her window, a low ceiling of clouds filled the slate-gray sky. As she began making coffee, it struck her that Bree was right when she described their lives as "unrecognizable." Their world had been cleaved in two. But they couldn't stop fighting now, not when they had a legitimate shot at getting some answers.

They knew the probate case would be an intense battle, so they enlisted a strong legal team. They hired Mike Jones, chair of the litigation department of Ivey, Barnum, and O'Mara, a well-respected Greenwich firm, and Eugene Riccio, a well-known criminal defense attorney.

Jennifer's probate team came from Middletown, near Cromwell, and primarily consisted of Richard Sheeley and Elizabeth Byrne.

Presiding over the case was Judge David Hopper, Greenwich born and raised, son of former probate judge Cameron Hopper, with whom he maintained a practice in town specializing in probate issues such as trusts, estates, and wills. David Hopper, a Republican, was active in the community as a member of several boards, including the First County Bank, the Transportation Association of Greenwich, and the Greenwich Old Timers Association. His Greenwich pedigree was classic.

But Hopper was already embroiled in a controversial case. An eighty-five-year-old woman named Marilyn Plank had been detained in a Greenwich assisted living facility for eighteen months, despite repeated pleas to the judge that she wished to return to Franklin, Michigan, where she was a legal resident. Describing her as a lifelong resident of Michigan, Hopper granted her plea to return to Franklin, but that decision took more than a year to make. The *Hartford Courant* called the case a "kidnapping, another warning of the injustice unfolding in this dangerous, antiquated judicial system."

The newspaper also reported that Probate Administrator Paul Knierim planned to investigate how Hopper had handled the Plank case.

---

When team Smith and team Hagel walked into chambers, the mood was uneasy. Maureen wore a look of grim determination as she joined George and their lawyers, Jones and Riccio. A contingent of print and television reporters also followed.

Then Jennifer arrived and made the rounds of the reporters and others in the waiting room at Hopper's chambers, introducing herself to everyone and cheerfully making conversation.

Frowning, Hopper let everyone in and described the proceedings as "informal." Jennifer smiled several times at Hopper, and he grinned back. With a nod to the informality of the mood, Hopper asked the parties to introduce themselves, which made the court proceedings seem more like a business brunch. Then he asked the press to leave because of confidentiality issues surrounding the case, including the possibility of future lawsuits. "It is critical to the future viability of this case to keep the facts of the case confidential until all of the lawsuits and/or potential appeals have been concluded," he said.

———

Jennifer began her testimony by describing the couple's promising beginnings. "The relationship sort of took off very quickly," she said. "We didn't get the whole Newport plan together, but we were excited, and George was saying, 'You know what? I'm just going to work at the store and make the best of it, you know. I'm going to just make it my own, maybe computerize things and do things.'"

After getting engaged, the couple moved into their apartment in the Byram section of Greenwich. "It was a cute place, and we just, you know, decorated it nice, and we had a patio set and a grill, and we were just, you know, sort of doing what most normal in-love couples do—like cooking, drinking great wine, having a great time, thinking our lives were pretty much perfect, especially when I got my teaching offer. It just seemed like everything was falling into place."

Hearing the news that George had visited a psychiatrist, Jennifer said, "I was actually proud of him. I felt like this is a young guy who—we're getting married, he's being proactive. He's saying, 'This is a problem, I want to take care of it.'"

Dr. Cooper, the psychiatrist, prescribed Zoloft and clonazepam. Jennifer testified that she didn't know where George kept his prescription drugs in their Greenwich apartment and that she had never seen him take them before or after the cruise. Her understanding was that "he was taking it the way you are supposed to be taking it, which would have been daily for the one, and that it was having a positive effect," she said. After the cruise, all the medication was accounted for, and no more pills were missing than should have been in George's prescription bottles, she added.

During the trial, Jones asked Jennifer to read a statement from Dr. Cooper, which said that George's "behavior has been stable and uneventful . . . medication compliance is good, rules are respected . . . no side effects are reported or in evidence."

Returning to her description of her honeymoon, Jennifer said the first two days in Barcelona were "awesome. We had a blast. Our whole trip is consisting of . . . dining out at the greatest restaurants . . . not a care in the world about anything. We are shopping, we are just eating out, drinking. George is, you know, waking up hung over and then starting again. But who cares, it was our honeymoon . . . And that was sort of like how every day was going."

Jennifer described the cruise as "not fully glamorous. You put on your life preserver, get out there with a gazillion people, typical cruise. As soon as we're done with all that . . . we're in pure vacation (mode), no care in the world. And music starts playing and the cruise ship sails and everyone on the ship is doing the same thing."

They met a young couple, Paul and Galina, who also liked to gamble in the casino at night, Jennifer said. They were gravitating toward the younger passengers, of which there were not many. "It wasn't like a Carnival cruise, where you tend to have a younger crowd." Another of the younger passengers was Josh Askin, whom Jennifer said they met in Italy with his family. Askin was in on the plan for George to smuggle a bottle of absinthe onboard the ship, she said.

Jennifer recounted the last day of George's life, on Mykonos Island. Back on the ship, the couple got ready for dinner. At Chops, they enjoyed "a beautiful meal, nice bottle of wine . . . and Irish coffee." But then Jennifer felt ill and "[threw] up my whole meal." After vomiting, she said she felt much better, so she and George went to the casino.

"We were playing craps or blackjack, sometimes together, sometimes separate, like our normal routine," she said. It was in the casino that Jennifer said she started "to lose time and not remember things . . . I remember going to the revolving door and thinking that the bar is spinning . . . and then a sense of tiredness or a sense of that—and that's really all I remember."

She said she remembered seeing the casino manager, Lloyd Botha, whom she described as "our favorite casino dealer . . . George and Lloyd are kind of like buddies." George would greet him by saying, "Hey, Lloyd Banks," the real name of rapper 50 Cent. Jennifer remembered noticing that Botha was "not there as a dealer, but he was there as sort of off duty. So that's why it stands out in my mind."

"I just remember being just tired, or I have to go home, or I'm standing up, but I'm—then that's it." She admitted later that "I got drunk" and "I blacked out."

She went blank until the next morning, when she woke up alone "in my same, you know, dress." The first thing she remembered was the massage appointment. She thought George perhaps had too much to drink and crashed in Paul and Galina's cabin. "I remember thinking, *See what happens, you drink too much, I am going to go to my massage, you're going to miss yours, and they're going to charge you anyway.*"

It didn't occur to her that anything in the cabin was amiss. After viewing images of it later, she commented, "The room looks a little messy. But we're halfway through the trip and this was—our room looks lived in."

The couples massage was scheduled for 10:00 a.m., but Jennifer arrived alone an hour and a half early for the appointment.

When ship officials interrupted her massage and told her the news that George was missing, the distraught and disoriented Jennifer was taken to the ship's lobby. She said Mrs. Askin hugged her and ship officials gave her a pill to calm her down. "They'll always say, 'We didn't tell her to do this, and we didn't tell her to do that,'" she said. "What I remember is someone saying or suggesting 'Do you want to take a shower, do you want something?'"

She was taken off the ship to an "office off the dock." Here she saw "people I recognized from the night before or just familiar faces from the cruise ship . . . And I remember all of them looking at me, like 'Wow, this is horrible . . . this is awful.'"

At the Turkish police station, in the "seedy . . . Third World country," she was accompanied by Marie Breheret, the ship's guest relations manager, and an "FBI consulate" who happened to be on vacation with his wife. Then a doctor "lifts up my shirt and looks down [my] pants," she said.

Her father collected her at Kennedy Airport in New York City, and Jennifer said she asked her father if they were going to stop at the Smiths. "'No, we're going home; everyone is tired.'"

Meanwhile, "the media is everywhere. They were leaving plants at the front door, leaving cards. Barbara Walters and every major media person wants to talk to you . . ." After returning, she claimed that she voluntarily took a polygraph test with the New Haven FBI.

Her testimony also illuminated the backchannel communication that led to her settlement after meeting Goldstein on *Oprah*. She e-mailed him herself, not through Walker. Walker "thought it was a little bizarre . . . He thought it was a little bit like playing. He just said, 'I've never had this sort of situation before.' I don't think he ever had a client that actually had interactions and communications directly with—he said, 'It's never happened before.'"

"Is it fair to say Royal Caribbean was worried about its public image?" asked Jones, the Smiths' lawyer.

"Sure, definitely for sure," said Jennifer.

"Do you agree that Royal Caribbean would place a high value on eliminating the publicity that this case was receiving?"

"Yes. How high, I don't know."

"At this point, I mean, they had Congress breathing down their necks, correct?"

"Yes, and they still do."

Jones asked Jennifer about a meeting with the FBI that included Assistant U.S. Attorney Peter Jongbloed. "Do you recall Mr. Jongbloed actually interjecting and looking right at you and saying, 'Jennifer, we also believe there was foul play,' meaning the Department of Justice and the FBI?"

Jennifer disagreed at first but eventually conceded that an FBI agent told her he didn't rule out foul play or an accident. "But the fact of the matter is in his mind that it was 50–50," she said. "He said, 'If we didn't think that there was a possibility of foul play, or something, then we wouldn't be investigating this.'"

Jones noted that Jennifer's statement was an apparent departure from her previous beliefs, as stated to Congress at the first Shays hearing in December 2005, in which she blasted

Royal Caribbean for characterizing George's death as an accident. Then she described how, when seeking representation in her lawsuit, "attorney after attorney that we saw gave us earfuls and earfuls that this is the seediest industry that you'll ever find, that there is a dark side to the cruise ship industry."

"And now you're giving them flowery accolades in the press," Jones said, pointing out that now her settlement hinged on "trusting this corporate felon to be honest and forthright in connection with turning over the documents you seek."

"Well, as you know, I'm a very positive person, OK?" Jennifer replied. "I always see the glass as half full. I'm not a pessimist. And as angry and frustrating as the situation has been, I fully believe—you know, I want to believe—that they are going to do all this. So am I naive? I hope not."

"Do you want me to answer that question?" asked Jones.

"No," said Jennifer.

She also knew that Royal Caribbean withheld privileged documents that the FBI requested, which Jones used to make a point about her "quick" settlement.

"We find out from the FBI that there are some privileged documents—or documents that Royal Caribbean has which they claim are privileged or work products. So from our standpoint it seems that would raise some sort of red flag, that why would—we don't understand why Royal Caribbean would hold these things back. The conceivable answer is that Royal Caribbean is hiding something. If they are hiding something, how can you so quickly settle with them?"

When Walker took the stand, his testimony diverged from Jennifer's. "If he [George] fell off the ship because of his intoxication, and there are pundits and newspaper articles suggesting he was sitting on the balcony smoking a cigar, I don't believe it. . . . My belief, I think there was foul play. I have always thought that. . . . I say it was 100 percent foul play."

Walker cited the four persons of interest in the case and cited a letter from Walker to Robert Peltz, a Royal Caribbean lawyer, which also shows his concern with the four men during a discussion of Dr. Lee's plans to visit *Brilliance of the Seas*. "Dr. Lee needs to walk from the cabin to the elevator and then to the cabins of Joshua Askin, Zachary Rozenberg, Gregory Rozenberg, and Rostislav Kofman. . . . Please provide us with their keycard/door activity reports for July 5, 2005, which we have requested many times."

Walker described the George Smith case as different from others he had represented because there was "information" in this one. "We've had cases where we've represented passengers and crew members who, quote, 'disappeared,'" he said. "I mean, there's no evidence, and you don't really know what happened. Here there's information that's pointing to four individuals. Now, if we're going to depose them, they're going to take the Fifth Amendment. They're not going to cooperate. Their counsel has made that clear."

"Their taking the Fifth Amendment has some potential use in a civil case, I assume?" asked Riccio, the Smiths' attorney.

"It could, sure," Walker replied.

Walker also blamed the Smiths for giving potential ammunition to the lawyers for some of the persons of interest in the case by cutting ties with Jennifer. When Walker was questioned about the wrongful death suit he filed on Jennifer's behalf—which described "blood in the bathroom, marks on the balcony window, and overturned furniture on the balcony" among other forensic evidence of foul play—he replied, "There was some overturned furniture, some marks on a balcony piece of glass, but the blood in the bathroom was Jennifer's makeup, which they took."

"So some of these allegations are not correct?" asked Riccio.

"Yeah, I think I was reaching with those, to be honest with you, with some of them," he said. But he maintained, "More probably than not, I think it was foul play . . . I think they [Royal Caribbean] were negligent . . . I think if he was in fact murdered, we know it was one of those four men. And I think that's why they paid what they paid at the end of the day, because they didn't want this case proceeding. I think they were also paying some publicity on top of it."

Riccio asked if there was a public relations benefit for Royal Caribbean to resolve the case.

"Sure," Walker replied. "There have been three hearings directly as a result of the Smiths' initial efforts. There's legislation that's been passed . . . it was on every show every night . . . And I think the cruise line is still suffering."

Walker also revealed that "Royal Caribbean made it . . . a prerequisite that the Smiths not be present" during Jennifer's settlement talks with the cruise line.

In another twist, Walker placed a multimillion-dollar price tag on the settlement value of the estate, between $3 and $6 million according to testimony by Maureen Smith. Jennifer also said, "I don't recall, but I think the idea was that it could be a multimillion-dollar case." And yet she settled for just $1.1 million, perhaps to end the negative publicity.

John Hagel testified about his doubts about the foul play theory. "I'm always open to the possibility of criminal activity or suspicious death, but maybe it's because of my background as a police officer [that] I've always been trained that the evidence will take you in a certain direction. You can't form, you know, she [Bree] formulated an end result which was the murder and cover-up theory with nothing to support it."

Hagel said that he and his family had three meetings with the FBI. "I never concluded anything. I just felt, based on the lack of evidence, that it probably, in my opinion, was not foul play." He also said that George's use of the prescription drugs was "very upsetting."

Under questioning from Jennifer's attorney, Elizabeth Byrne, Maureen said she wasn't aware of George's use of prescription drugs. She also said that George never called in late to work at the package store, never appeared "disheveled . . . or hung over . . . I never saw evidence of a drinking problem."

When Byrne showed her a photo and questioned her about the blood in the cabin—saying "the only blood in the room was this blood, this small spot, small splotch of blood, small splotch on the sheet"—Maureen said, "Maybe, by the time they got there, that was all that was there. I do know that the FBI removed the carpet from the cabin. Why would they remove the carpet from the cabin if they didn't think there was something on it?"

————

On May 8, Hopper announced that he had made his decision, upholding Jennifer's settlement.

> *After a review of the facts, and the applicable maritime, international, and domestic law, there is no way to possibly predict the result of any litigation associated with this case. Under some circumstances, it would be conceivable for the estate to recover nothing and be in debt due to the costs associated with fully and properly litigating the issues.*

His ruling prevented the Smiths from getting the information they wanted until they, too, settled. Hopper ruled that Jennifer had acted "prudently" in negotiating the agreement in June 2006. "One thing that is clear about this case is that there are no winners. Both parties have suffered a great loss, which will be with them for the rest of their lives."

"We are disappointed and frankly very surprised, based upon the way the evidence went in," Mike Jones said. "We do not agree with the court's findings and more than likely will be filing an appeal."

When the Smiths did file an appeal in Stamford Superior Court, Jennifer issued a press release once again putting forward an accidental-death theory. The press release said that she had "been forced to accept the likelihood that George's death was the result of a tragic accident" because of a mixture of alcohol and antidepressants. The records of the probate case were sealed, though, so this was the first anyone had heard of the Zoloft and clonazepam. Reports of blood evidence—which she had once listed in her lawsuit and testified about to Congress—she described as "baseless."

Rivkind described the press release as a classic case of the "best defense is a good offense . . . It's astounding, particularly in light of the views by Mr. Walker about how Mr. Smith died and the language in the complaint he was prepared to file against Royal Caribbean before Ms. Hagel Smith decided to settle."

And then the antidepressants hit the headlines. As the latest version of the story unfolded, John Hagel defended his daughter more vehemently than ever. He even called the *Greenwich Post* to elaborate on his probate court testimony.

Hagel claimed that his family's meetings with the FBI convinced them that there was "no blood evidence and no suspects in the case," despite previous FBI reports. Further, he said, original reports of blood evidence of foul play turned out to be "just specks, from maybe a pimple or Jennifer's makeup."

When asked about the charges in Jennifer's wrongful death lawsuit and Jennifer's congressional testimony, Hagel snapped that the information was dated. "The FBI has not got any indictments in two and a half years, and the grand jury didn't get any indictments. There is now no evidence of any foul play and no suspects."

There was no evidence now, but had there been?

Of Walker's contradictory statements, Hagel said that Walker was not at the FBI meetings, and he described Walker as having "a cynical nature."

Hagel then picked up the thread about George's reported mixture of alcohol and prescription drugs as "a recipe for disaster. That's taboo," he said.

When asked to comment on Hagel's statements, the usually unflappable Jones was silent for moment. "I am shocked that Mr. Hagel compromised the confidentiality of a criminal FBI investigation by speaking to the press about it."

———

Around this time, Jennifer's website was heavily revised. Gone were the many references to "substantial evidence of foul play." Instead it read:

*Reward $100,000 for new information leading directly to the arrest and conviction of the individual or individuals responsible for the death of George Allen Smith IV, white male, 26, brown hair, blue eyes. George disappeared from Brilliance of the Seas, operated by Royal Caribbean during his honeymoon cruise on July 5, 2005, in the Mediterranean (Aegean Sea) between*

*Greece and Turkey and has been declared dead. The
reward will be paid by the estate of George A. Smith IV,
following the arrest and conviction of the individuals.*

The *Greenwich Post* asked both Sheeley and Walker why
the references to foul play were removed and why there is
even a need for a website to collect tips and information if
George likely died from a tragic accident. Neither Sheeley
nor Walker responded.

Meanwhile, the *Greenwich Post* won a freedom-of-
information request to unseal the probate transcript in order
to cover the highly publicized case fairly and objectively. In
his decision to unseal the case, Judge Hopper wrote that he
had initially cited a need for confidentiality because of future
lawsuits in the case. But he had decided to make them public
in an attempt to "balance constitutional rights and the best
interests of the estate." He also said he was concerned about
the way "the adminstratrix [Jennifer] in the case was cherry
picking information in the transcript to be made public."

When the records were unsealed, the media seized on the
controversy surrounding the foul play theory, quoting Walker's
belief in it, and the description of the exchange between
Jennifer and Jongbloed, which also gave it further credence.
Nearly every headline bore the phrase "foul play possible in
cruise case," from the AP story to television news reports.

In August 2009 the Hagels issued a press release announcing Jennifer's engagement to Jeff Agne, indicating that the wedding would take place at a Vermont resort in October. "We couldn't be happier," John Hagel told the Associated Press. "We're just thrilled she's been able to move on with her life and start a new life with Jeff."

Jennifer was still working at the Michael J. Fox Foundation, and on their website her name had changed to Jennifer Hagel-Agne.

# 18

# GLIMMERS OF HOPE

In California, Laurie Dishman, who claimed she had been brutally raped on a Royal Caribbean cruise, read an article about the George Smith case that mentioned ICV. It galvanized her to step forward, she said in an interview with the *Greenwich Citizen*. Her case was the final arrow ICV needed in its quiver.

To celebrate their thirty-year-friendship, Laurie and Michelle, who met when they were five years old—decided to take a Royal Caribbean cruise to the Mexican Riviera, relaxing poolside in the sun, umbrella drinks in hand.

"We were having so much fun," said Dishman. But on the night of February 21, her life changed forever.

While Laurie and Michelle were toasting their friendship in the Viking Lounge, a crewmember whose badge read SECURITY GUARD approached them. According to Dishman, he demanded to see their IDs and asked whether they were old enough to be drinking in the bar. He also asked for their cabin number. Believing him trustworthy, they gave it to him.

The night of talking and dancing continued, and when Dishman got up to request a song from the deejay, the same crewmember approached her again. Dishman claims he held her wrist and kissed her while trying to whisper something in her ear.

"No, get away!" Dishman said.

The incident disturbed Dishman and prompted her to leave the lounge with Michelle to avoid the crewman's alleged unwanted advances. They returned to their cabin. Michelle knew her friend was upset, so she waited for Laurie to fall asleep before she went back to the lounge.

Later that night, a knock at the door woke Laurie. Thinking it was Michelle, who wasn't in the cabin, she opened the door halfway. According to Dishman, the crewman shoved his way into the room and pushed her onto the bed. She struggled, but he squeezed his hands around her neck and raped her. Then he left her, passed out on the bed, with dark brown and red ligature marks around her neck where he had choked her.

She woke the following morning to a conundrum. Her alleged rapist was supposedly security, so Laurie asked Michelle, who had returned to the room while Laurie slept, who should they call? They rang the purser's desk, and two officers arrived at their cabin soon after.

But instead of securing the cabin as a crime scene, Laurie claims the officers sat on her bed. They questioned her about the allegations in her stateroom, where evidence may have been compromised, and at one point, she said, one crewman told her, "You need to control your drinking." Eventually they allowed Dishman to go to the ship's doctor, but this led to another startling twist.

"He told Michelle and me to go back to our cabin and collect the sheets and clothing from the incident and to place them in plastic bags, which they had provided. The entire process was so humiliating."

Worse, even though she was able to identify her alleged assailant, he continued to work aboard the ship. After collecting the evidence herself, she asked the captain if she could go home because she knew the crewmember was still onboard.

The two women flew to Los Angeles, where the FBI interviewed them. "We were informed that the FBI was taking this matter 'very seriously' and we actually believed they were."

Back home, Laurie received a call from the FBI, who informed her that the Department of Justice wasn't going to prosecute her case. "They said that it was a 'he said/she said' case. I felt violated all over again."

Dishman said she later learned that the DOJ declined the case for prosecution and that the FBI closed the "investigation" on the same day that the cruise ship returned to port, before anyone began a serious effort to investigate the crime. Compounding her fears, Royal Caribbean refused to provide her with the name, address, nationality, or whereabouts of her alleged assailant.

Instead she says she received a bizarre promotional letter from Royal Caribbean: "Thank you for sailing with us and giving us the opportunity to send you home with an experience to remember." The letter contained a discount coupon.

Royal Caribbean disputed Dishman's claims and told the *Los Angeles Times* that the company has an "enviable safety record," with millions of Americans vacationing without incident on cruises each year. Gary Bald, senior vice president of global security for Royal Caribbean Cruises Ltd., told the *Greenwich Citizen* that the company improved security and took steps to "ensure that in the future, victims are given better information and support and crime scenes are secured. . . . It was our intention and desire to assist Laurie Dishman in every way we could," Bald said. "I feel we accomplished that in some respects but in others I feel we came up short."

In March 2006 Dishman read a *Time* magazine article that discussed the George Smith case and ICV. It also mentioned the alleged rape of Janet Kelly, whose case bore many similarities to hers, and how Kelly had stepped forward to testify before Congress.

"I realized I wasn't alone," she said.

She joined ICV and hired James Walker to sue Royal Caribbean. Then she wrote to her congresswoman, Doris Matsui.

---

On March 27, 2007, Dishman joined Ken Carver and testified in a third round of congressional hearings, hoping to get the stalled cruise safety bill moving again.

Sensing another imbroglio in Washington, the cruise industry swung into action.

On the eve of the hearings, CLIA's Terry Dale announced a new, voluntary agreement with the FBI and the Coast Guard to report any serious crimes committed onboard cruise ships. But Shays pointed out that a voluntary agreement wasn't strong enough. "Cruise ship crime victims must be able to share information and warn others. The industry's agreement to report crimes to the FBI voluntarily is a step forward, but it's not enough. Under this agreement, there is no enforcement and no laws to ensure it complies. Educating the public, members of Congress, and the media is the only way to improve cruise ship safety."

As the hearings opened under the chairmanship of Congressman Elijah Cummings of Maryland, Congresswoman Matsui took a strong stand, giving ICV a powerful new ally. After hearing Dishman's story, Matsui said she had discovered that "there is no shortage of rape, sexual assault, alcohol-related abuse, or man-overboard cases on America's cruise lines. This is alarming in and of itself. However, what is even more troubling is that most of these incidents are never fully resolved or prosecuted."

The testimonials began with Carver, explaining ICV's ten-point plan. But Congressman Mica kept interrupting, questioning the need for it. "I have an analogy," Carver said, exasperated. "Let's say this is the Aviation Committee of the U.S. Congress, and an airline came to this committee and said, 'We have a new business plan. We're going to license the company in Liberia because that's very helpful. We don't have to pay federal income tax. We're going to staff with Third World people, but we want to fly out of New York City. We want to fly out of New York City; we want to fly out of Los Angeles. Once that airplane takes off, hey, we've got a whole different set of rules. You may not understand them, but trust us. Now, over the past year, we've lost twenty-eight passengers, disappeared. We've had a couple hundred people raped, but trust us.' Would you think the American public would allow that airline to be licensed in this country to fly out of their major airports?"

Mica avoided the point or missed it entirely. "Well, again, we do have very similar situations in aviation, and we do have many incidents, some reported and unreported."

Then Dishman took the stand, recounting her ordeal. She urged the adoption of increased safety measures on cruise ships as proposed by the ICV, including the presence and use of sea marshals and mandatory background checks for crewmembers. She also said that foreign-flagged cruise ships should be forced to register in the United States and follow U.S. laws. "Otherwise, they are like small cities with no laws."

When she was done, she took a deep breath and looked at the congressional panel. "I am the next Janet Kelly. Please don't let there be another Laurie Dishman."

After a moment of silence, Congressman Cummings gestured toward Terry Dale and the other industry officials. "I promise you," he said. "If there is breath in my body, you will be back."

---

The Dishman story at the latest round of hearings fueled more press coverage. In August, Walker fanned the frenzy by releasing e-mails that showed just how worried the cruise industry was about the Dishman case. The e-mails were between Alan Wilson, editor and publisher of *Cruise News Daily,* a daily online newsletter that favors the cruise industry, and Michael Sheehan, associate vice president of corporate communications for Royal Caribbean. They contained a shockingly callous exchange.

Wilson to Sheehan: "I really want to nail this woman—and the ICV."

"Let's see what we can do tomorrow!!!!" Sheehan replied.

Wilson also published an article about the Dishman case in his newsletter questioning the veracity of some of her claims, which Dishman described as "mocking."

But Dishman's courage resonated. On April 9, 2008, the Congressional Victims Rights Caucus gave her their Unsung Hero Award, presented to a crime victim or survivor who uses his or her experiences "to promote public education and awareness, public policy, development, and/or greater awareness about crime victims' rights and needs."

"Laurie Dishman is truly a hero," said Matsui, who introduced the Protect Americans from Crimes on Cruise Ships Resolution on September 17, 2007, along with Shays and Congresswoman Carolyn Maloney of New York. More than thirty representatives cosponsored it in the House of Representatives.

The ICV had its momentum in the House, but they kept running into roadblocks in the Senate, where no one would step forward to sponsor the bill. Then Ken Carver suggested they ask John Kerry, who had represented his daughter Merrian, a resident of Cambridge, Massachusetts. After hearing the ICV's stories, Kerry agreed to hold the hearing on June 19, 2008.

Called "Cruise Ship Safety: Examining Potential Steps for Keeping Americans Safe at Sea," it fell under the auspices of the Surface Transportations and Merchant Marine Subcommittee. It was the first Senate hearing in the industry's sixty-year history.

Carver had done his homework. He told ICV's story, how it had grown from just the Smith family and himself to include members throughout the United States and in twenty countries across the globe. ICV had allied with organizations such as the National Organization of Parents of Murdered Children; the National Center for Victims of Crimes; the Rape, Abuse, and Incest National Network; and Crime Victims United of California.

To tell the story of Merrian's disappearance, Carver brought every document and every shred of correspondence. He also brought new ammunition, including a poll about cruise crime conducted by the website cruisecritic.com. The poll, conducted a little more than a year before the Senate hearing, attempted to determine how many people had been affected by cruise crimes. Of the 1,700 people questioned, 10 percent said they had been affected by a cruise crime. Ross Klein calculated that this figure suggested that "as many as one million Americans may be the victim of a crime on a cruise ship."

Carver also raised the specter of terrorism, citing the need for the equivalent of sky marshals onboard because of this threat. Then Carver painted a picture of the Goliath industry that ICV was challenging. "They say they have zero tolerance for crimes, but CLIA has yet to commit in writing to any changes." They also "aggressively oppose any changes, with the backing of the $2.8 million they spent in federal lobbying in 2007. Compare that to the $280,000 that Wal-Mart spent."

Kerry, the normally stoic New Englander, looked increasingly disturbed. He sharply questioned Terry Dale, who appeared beleaguered. After the hearings, Kerry agreed to sponsor the bill in the Senate.

"Millions of Americans will board cruise ships this year, and they should know that they are safe," he said. "The tragic loss of Ken Carver's daughter, Merrian, should serve as a reminder that security and crime reporting regulations need to be tightened. Murky legal jurisdictions in international waters are no longer an excuse for failing to report serious crimes so that they may be effectively prosecuted."

The final piece of the puzzle had fallen into place.

Kerry's hearing and sponsorship of the bill spawned more headlines and news reports. The cruise industry dropped its battle against the bill. Toxic headlines were eclipsing the launch of their mammoth new ships, and like most stocks during the economic downturn, the value of their stocks continued to slide. *Bloomberg News* reported a "sales slump" for Royal Caribbean, saying its projected 2009 profit "will fall more than analysts estimated." The cruise line slashed ticket prices to stimulate demand, but shares still dropped 13 percent.

"We're terribly disappointed at the kind of pricing levels that we have to offer in this market," Fain said. "Until a few months ago, we were doing substantially better."

By July 2009 the cruise industry looked ready to fold its hand. Terry Dale sent a letter to Kerry saying he would "work to ensure the passage of the comprehensive security bill," marking a complete reversal of CLIA's stance on government oversight.

———

On a hot July day a year later, President Obama signed the historic Cruise Vessel Security and Safety Act into law. The bill requires mandatory reporting of crimes. Cruise ship personnel must now contact both the FBI and the Coast Guard as soon as a homicide, suspicious death, missing U.S. citizen, kidnapping, assault, or other serious occurrence is reported. The cruise industry also must comply with several new security provisions, including the installation of forty-two-inch guardrails, new peepholes in every passenger and crewmember's door, and the use of on-deck video surveillance. All ships must have a logbook to record all deaths, missing individuals, alleged crimes, thefts, sexual harassment, and assault. Crewmembers are required to be trained in crime prevention, detection, evidence preservation, and reporting. Rape kits must be available and a trained forensic sexual assault specialist must travel on each ship.

The act takes effect on January 1, 2012. Ships that fail to comply face strict penalties. Civil penalties include fines up to $50,000, and criminal penalties, defined as "willful" violations, can result in up to $250,000 in fines, a year in jail, or both. Most prohibitive to the industry, ships may be denied entry to U.S. ports for noncompliance with the new law.

Senator Kerry and Ken Carver, among many others in Washington, D.C., hailed the landmark bill. The Smiths followed the news from Greenwich. Five years had passed since George's disappearance upended their lives. They found a modicum of comfort in the passage of the act. The family was keeping mostly to itself, focusing on the upcoming appeal of the probate decision in Stamford Superior Court.

Chris Shays didn't attend the celebration either, having been defeated in 2008 in the blue sweep of the Obama election. But for the Smith family he was there in spirit. "We will never forget that Mr. Shays brought the need for reform of the cruise industry to the national spotlight and was a crusader for George, our family, and all the other cruise crime victims that had been silenced for so long," Bree said.

Jennifer Hagel-Agne made no public statement about the act.

———

The following September, the Smiths reached a settlement with both Royal Caribbean and Jennifer. Royal Caribbean agreed to give them new information that would shed new light on the case. Mike Jones made the announcement, telling the press that the new agreement "expands the scope of the information obtained from Royal Caribbean" and "hopefully provides the FBI with additional information for their investigation into George's disappearance." The amount of the settlement with Royal Caribbean, $1.31 million, approximates "the projected earnings of George during his lifetime."

Jones underscored, however, that the FBI investigation was still open and active.

Under the settlement, Royal Caribbean is required to furnish "comprehensive information" to the Smiths, including witness statements made to Royal Caribbean by those individuals last seen with George and from Royal Caribbean employees.

Unlike Jennifer's, the Smiths' agreement was not confidential. "This agreement allows for the settlement terms and the documentation obtained from Royal Caribbean from their investigation into George's death to be made public," Jones announced. "There is no requirement of confidentiality." When the FBI finishes its review, the Smiths plan to go public with the new information.

Richard Sheeley, Jennifer's lawyer, said she was "pleased that we were finally able to bring some measure of closure to this long-litigated matter. . . . All Jennifer ever wanted was to get all available information from Royal Caribbean to provide some explanation for George's disappearance and we simply hope that, despite the amount of time that has passed with this litigation, any trail that may have existed is not so cold as to produce answers."

Maureen Smith had stronger words. "Our goal from the beginning of this litigation was to find out what happened to George and bring his perpetrators to justice. This settlement brings us one step closer to achieving our objective."

The $1.31 million would put a dent in but not "cover the expenditures that George and Maureen incurred in legal and investigative efforts to find out who killed George over five years ago," Jones said. Those efforts include the depositions of "the individuals last seen with George, some of whom have invoked their Fifth Amendment rights." The family was pleased to have the litigation behind them, but "their battle has not ended."

———

The four men of interest in the case found their lives deeply shadowed by the George Smith case and their names splashed across the news wires and the Internet.

Josh Askin earned a degree in marketing from San Diego State University in 2008. On his Facebook page he lists his status as "in a relationship with Leigh Georgis." Askin is listed as the drummer for San Diego band Mad Martigan on their Facebook page.

Rostislav "Rusty" Kofman is reportedly attending law school in New York City.

His cousin, Zach Rozenberg, earned a degree in business and management.

Gregory Rozenberg sank into a downward spiral that led to an arrest for heroin trafficking in Palm Beach County in 2009. Housed in close confinement, he is serving a three-year sentence in the Florida maximum-security prison that once held serial killers Ted Bundy, Aileen Wuornos, and Ottis Toole. In the prison website photo, Gregory has shaved his blond hair and is wearing a black prison jumpsuit and white undershirt. He stares without expression into the camera.

## About the Author

Joan Lownds, a reporter for the *Greenwich Citizen* and the *Greenwich Post,* has been covering the story of the George Smith murder since it broke. She is an award-winning writer and reporter for several Connecticut newspapers and magazines, including the *Litchfield County Times, Newtown Bee, New Haven Advocate, Yale Alumni* magazine, and *New England* magazine. She lives in Naugatuck, Connecticut.